Like His
Brothers
and Sisters

Therefore
he had to become like his brothers and
sisters in every respect, so that he
might be a merciful and faithful high
priest in the service of God, to make a
sacrifice of atonement for the sins of
the people. Because he himself was
tested by what he suffered, he is able
to help those who are being tested.

(Hebr 2:17)

Like His Brothers and Sisters

■

ORDAINING COMMUNITY LEADERS

FRITZ LOBINGER

A Crossroad Faith & Formation Book
The Crossroad Publishing Company
New York

First published in 1998 in the Philippines by Claretian Publications.

Published in the United States in 1999 by The Crossroad Publishing Company, 370 Lexington Avenue, New York, NY 10017.

Printed in the Philippines

Library of Congress Catalog Card Number: 99-066574

ISBN: 0-8245-1831-4

1 2 3 4 5 6 7 8 9 10   04 03 02 01 00 99

Contents

Introduction

This short study is about the proposed ordination of proven leaders of Catholic communities. This suggestion is usually made under the technical Latin term of "viri probati" – meaning "proven men". The term refers to the married proven leaders of Catholic communities that have no priest. Our study reflects on this question in a slightly different way. While most people begin their considerations with a reminder of the shortage of priests, we would like to take a different starting point.

About our great leader from Nazareth it was said: "Therefore he had to become like his brothers and sisters in every respect, so that he might be a merciful and faithful high priest in the service of God, to make a sacrifice of atonement for the sins of the people. Because he himself was tested by what he suffered, he is able to help those who are being tested." (Hebr 2:17)

Our priests of today are human beings like all of us, but they are still quite dissimilar. They do not live from the work of their hands. They do not have a family. Must all our ordained leaders be of that kind? Could we introduce a second kind of priest who is living in a way similar to the rest of the community? Questions such as these are at the heart of this study.

Many have already suggested that the ordination of community leaders or "viri probati" is the solution. Frequently we have heard the opinion that the introduction of such ordinations simply depends on the courage of some bishops to demand this step. They also think that all that is needed is a change in the present legislation which would allow the ordination of such leaders to the ministerial priesthood.

Even among the bishops, one can notice that those who are for the introduction of ordained community leaders are aware of only very few implications such a move will have, and similarly that those who are *against* know rather little about the implications which they fear and which prompt them to oppose such a move. The lack of clarity on both sides makes it doubtful that the positions presently taken are based on sound judgment.

All of us need to understand the chain reaction which is likely to follow the introduction of ordained community leaders in order to make up our mind. Even those who sense that such a step is necessary are unlikely to ask for it officially unless they are certain this can be done in a responsible way. For this reason the present study was prepared. Many more studies of this nature are needed, as each person and each group sees the situation in a different way.

There is an urgent need to reflect on these questions because, while the demand for introducing ordained community leaders is intensifying, at the same time the quality of argumentation for or *against* is not improving. Among the many publications which call for the ordination of community leaders there are a good number which seem unaware of the serious dangers inherent in the way they foresee such a step to be initiated. The experience of other Churches proves that not every method of "tent-maker ministry" will produce good results.

It is therefore vital to stimulate reflection on these questions. A long delay can lead to a situation where the shortage of priests becomes so severe that the leaders of the Church are suddenly prepared to opt for "panic ordinations" which can cause great harm for a long time to come. This study is being published so that its ideas can be shared with others. All the aspects outlined in it would still require much more detail. We could only sketch each area that will be affected by such a change in ministry, and offer the most likely way in which each problem might be dealt with. Further study papers are needed which aim at fuller detail.

In Part One we begin by showing how different the situations are from which the call for the ordination of *viri probati* is presently coming. These situations differ so much that one realizes that the various areas may have to choose different paths to reach the same goal. In Part Two we list the different forms under which the ordination of viri probati has been suggested until now and will try to show that we should adopt only one of these options. In the rest of Part Two we introduce not only one new kind of priest but two, and show that having two kinds of priest is not a problem but rather part of the solution.

Part Three sketches the most likely way in which this option would unfold. It is based on the option of ordaining not single operators but teams of local leaders interacting with teams of animator priests. It foresees how the start could be made, how the various parts of the Church will react, which dangers would have to be avoided and how feasible this proposal will be.

This publication hopes to encourage others to draft similar studies, to form study groups on this topic, and to compare their reflections. The author is aware that in such questions one has to rely on attempts to make predictions and how uncertain these are. This makes it all the more important that others will make different attempts and compare their ideas. A decision will have to be made one day, and it would best be based on the comparison of the different ways of seeing the future.

Part One

The Call for the Ordination of Community Leaders Comes from very different situations

The idea to ordain proven married local leaders – called "viri probati" – has been voiced in many ways and by different groups. This was proposed by groups of bishops during the Second Vatican Council, it was proposed by many individual writers, it was raised by conferences of pastoral workers and by groups of priests and groups of lay people; it was demanded by several diocesan synods and in many countries. There seems to be a united chorus asking for the same solution in the same situation of a shortage of priests.

The dramatic decrease in the number of priests has been demonstrated by a multitude of publications. They have shown how in many parts of the Church the faithful are starved of the Eucharist, how this is eroding the traditional Catholic love for the sacraments and that the shortage of priests has many other negative side effects. Many authors have explained that communities have a right to the sacraments and a right to have a priest. The conclusion has always been the same: the trend towards an increasingly serious shortage of priests is almost universal, is certain to continue, and can be solved only by a change in the admission criteria to the ministerial priesthood. Practically all authors are pointing out that the solution is to be found less in admitting married candidates for full-time priesthood, but rather in ordination of members of the local community, the "viri probati". One can observe a great unanimity in taking the shortage of priests as the starting point, and ordination of local leaders as the conclusion.

It is only when one considers the details how such a proposal could be implemented that one begins to realize that the situations from which this unanimous call is emanating are quite different. One then begins to see that these differences are not just minor but are essential. It then dawns on us that there is not just one magic solution for all these situations. It could even be dangerous to simply proceed and ordain *viri probati* in all those parts of the Church which ask for it.

Let us therefore acquaint ourselves of some of the different situations from which this proposal emanates. We will describe only the main categories of parishes and communities without mentioning the many in-between types and shades. Our purpose is not the exact description of all details, but to raise awareness of the differences and contrasts. The discussion of the ordination of *viri probati* can be conducted only as a world-wide dialogue, because the decision of one part of the Church on this question will unavoidably touch all others. No part of the Church should therefore consider only its own situation.

Starved of the Eucharist

Only bicycles can pass along the highway between Cazombo and Luwawo. Destruction and decay are everywhere: broken bridges, high grass, pot-holes made by landmines, fallen trees. Such is the scene in this part of war-torn Angola.

I and my companions, three catechists, cycled during the day. We had to get off and push on the sandy, swampy paths and the small hills, most of the time under a hot sun or through strong, rainy gales. When it was too sunny, clouds would gather and protect us and when it became unbearably hot the clouds would open up and cool us with a shower.

Angola is a beautiful country, full of rivers, grand panoramas and lovely scenery, with birds and animals and snakes of various kinds. As we cycled along in the open air or enclosed by the thick forest, the birds whose territories we were crossing welcomed us with their melodies.

It would have been easier to go to Luwawo by air, as others do, but I wanted to meet the communities along the way at their Sunday assemblies. These assemblies are made up of returning exiles and people who never left. Together in their need they strive to find Christ.

Our first stop after a day and a half along the cycle path was at Mazoze, the former guerrilla base. Most of the fighters now live there in retirement with their families. The old, the young and the newly-born make up a complex community.

Two of the older folk told me they had not seen a priest since 1961. One or two women were astonished, looking at me and then pulling a face in amazement, pondering: "Is it possible, a priest visiting us? Is this really happening?" For them the eucharistic celebration of bygone years had become only a sweet memory. Now it lived again and all felt the eucharistic Christ strongly in their midst. An elderly catechist had kept the flock together, through war and peace. It could truly be said of him: "Well done, good and faithful servant." Our catechists have been consistent and daring in teaching and preaching. I admire the way they reflect and suggest good behaviour when I know they have no library and nobody to consult. Indeed, some of them are hardly able to read.

We moved on towards other "Sunday" assemblies. We saw main roads dug with trenches, trucks destroyed by landmines, burnt machinery. It was a reminder that 10 years ago, this beautiful country was a battle-field. We saw the results of accidents, too, such as the schoolboy who had found a hand-grenade and was playing with it with friends. When it exploded, one boy was killed on the spot and others were injured. An adult who found an anti-personnel mine had tried to examine it: even after plastic surgery, his face is disfigured.

As we entered the city of Luwawo in full moonlight at about 7 p.m., we met a good Samaritan, a Methodist, who went before us along the road announcing: "Padri weya. Padri weya, Katolika" ("Here is your priest. Come and meet him"). The people duly came out to welcome us. It will take years to restore the roads and bridges and to clear the fields of mines. The Christians of these Sunday assemblies, who have for so long proved their belief in Christ and his message, will remain cut off from easy communication and grow old without receiving the sacraments although this is their right.

No humanitarian agency is going to give me, or even consider the idea of giving me, a helicopter for pastoral work or an amphibious car to carry me and my Mass kit, yet the faithful of these Sunday assemblies have the right to all the sacraments. I am nearly 55 years of age. It would be unwise of me to cycle out on a two- or three-day safari each month to reach this flock. Nor would it be fair to call elderly catechists, on foot or on bicycle, to come to me so they could carry back the eucharistic bread.

In rebel-held territories in southern Sudan, it is the same story. Lacking a priest, the assembly leader keeps the faithful together. During the war in Mozambique, catechists in the war zones would walk eight days and then take a bus to reach the community in Malawi where I was working, so that they could carry the Eucharist back with them for their people. Is this necessary? Is there no end to their suffering?

Is the sacramental life necessary? An African moralist would say: "Educate them to live a good life without the sacraments" – a solution following the line of least resistance.

My pastoral concern reminds me of the words of Christ, "When two or three are gathered together in my name, I am in their midst" (Mt. 18, 20). This is a slight comfort, at least.

One or two African bishops entertain the vision of an auxiliary priesthood as a solution to this problem, but they also recognise the probable gap that would open up between the town priest and the village priest, the seminary-educated priest and the priest-catechist.

When we were baptised we were anointed with the oil of chrism, thus making us partakers in the priesthood of Christ. A pastoral canonist once suggested to me that for people in this emergency situation there is the possibility of the "priesthood of the assembly of the faithful." He meant that whenever an assembly is formed to celebrate the word of God, one of the elders could consecrate the host and wine *hic et nunc* and *toties quoties* ("here and now"' and "as often as the need arises"). This would require a consensus among the hierarchy.

I remember hearing in a theology lecture hall that the origin of the present eucharistic celebration was from the Acts of the Apostles (2:42): "They were faithful to the teaching of the Apostles, the common life of sharing, the breaking of bread and prayers." Surely the pastoral theologians, the biblical theologians, and liberation theologians should be asked to throw more light on this idea for the benefit of war victims living and dying without eucharistic food.

(S. F., THE TABLET, 10 May 1997)

A replying friend sees problems:

Sir, Fr. S. F.'s article (10 May) about his experiences in Angola was of particular interest to me. I worked in Angola from 1977 until 1991, with one year's sabbatical in the middle, and will be returning there in September.

For eight years I was one of the priests serving the diocese of Malanje, which is bigger than Scotland. For several years there were only twelve of us. Of its thirteen parishes or missions, two were run by nuns and three by catechists. After 1984, because of the war, six could not be visited by priests.

It is an anomaly that Christian communities, fervent in faith and facing great hostility, should be deprived of "the summit and source of Christian life." Another anomaly is the fact that huge amounts of money and effort are invested in seminaries, more than in any other single activity. I spent seven years full-time in a seminary. Most of those benefiting from this education and secure lifestyle do not actually become priests. Those who do receive an elevated status, much privilege and great power.

There is no obvious solution: instituting an "auxiliary priesthood" as Fr S. suggests, would not only mean creating a gap between such auxiliaries and the seminary-trained priesthood, but would bring clericalism into the heart of the village community; such is the image of priesthood in the

Catholic Church. Also, who would support the priest financially? Many communities have difficulty supporting even their catechists.

I think it is the type of priest, the image of priesthood, that has to change over the years. Perhaps one way to begin is to invest more in training the laity for different roles in the local community, where power is not with one single person, and eventually – years ahead – ordaining one of these to preside at the sacraments. This would mean investing less in seminaries. Yes, we need the theologians to think deeply, and the hierarchy to act boldly. And above all we need a profound change in the mindset of most priests, whereby they would shun privilege, share power, and be seen as servants.

Father J. F. (THE TABLET, 24 May 1997)

The community of Silungile is ready – waiting for the lawmakers

The Catholic community of Silungile is not easy to reach. You would have to travel by bus on bad roads for two hours to visit it and you would first have to find out on which days of the week the bus takes that route.

Neither is it easy for the priest to reach that community. What makes it difficult is not just the long journey and the bad roads but the fact that this is only one of the twenty-five similar communities he is serving, together with the other priest with whom he stays in the little town not too far away. This means that the community can have Mass only every second month, about six times a year.

Father is not happy about this situation of the infrequent celebration of the Eucharist but he is not too worried about the community of Silungile. The reason is that he knows there are many trained and reliable leaders in Silungile. He himself has trained them and he knows their reliability.

Yes, there are several kinds of leaders in Silungile, actually several teams of them. The most important group is that of the liturgy leaders. The group has grown to eight this year as two new ones have been trained and commissioned.

The liturgy leaders meet on Thursday evening to prepare the Sunday service. Actually the meeting begins with a short evaluation of the liturgy of the previous Sunday. This is the time when it is clarified which three of them will lead the service of the Word on the coming Sunday. Of course there is a roster for all the Sundays but there is always the possibility that a leader is sick or away in town or, for some other reason, is unable to function. The leaders make sure that there will be three of them to conduct the liturgy. A further purpose of coming together is to look at the text of the readings, to determine who will preach, who will confer with the hymn leaders, and who will ensure that the readers are acquainted with the texts so that they can prepare. If a funeral is to take place before the next meeting, leaders are appointed to conduct it.

Another important team is that of the catechism teachers. It consists mostly of younger women. As the Catholic community is quite large – approximately nine hundred, twelve women have been trained to teach catechism to the various age groups. Leaders of catechumen groups, numerous in former times when there was still a large number of catechumens, are not so many any more. The number of people who do not yet belong to any Church is quite small, thus reducing the number of catechumens.

One could not say that the people of Silungile are deeply unhappy about having the Eucharist only every second month. They are used to it. But they know it is not the real Catholic practice. They do not complain to the priest because they know that Father travels every day to visit the various communities and most of all on Sundays. They know how much time he gives to training sessions during the week, as well as celebrating Masses on Sundays.

They are not complaining but they have begun to wonder. During one of those long training meetings of two days they ask Father whether he thinks the bishop will one day have more priests and can appoint one to their village. Will that ever happen? Father says he doubts it. After talking it over for some time, they begin to understand. There will be some vocations among their young people, but they might be sufficient to just replace the existing priests as they grow older. There is no hope that they will ever increase to such an extent that the many distant villages will have their own priest. That is a futile dream. They are lucky to have even two priests for their rather large area; they cannot expect more.

The conversation does not end there. One of them surprisingly asks Father whether it will be absolutely impossible for them to be allowed to celebrate the sacraments on their own one day. He says that he read in the Bible how Paul appointed elders in all the many places where he founded new communities of believers. Is this not really possible today? Father replies that it is not envisaged at the moment but it is not entirely impossible in the future. He adds, however, that such a change in the legislation of the Church could not be made by only one diocese. It should be decided by the whole Church, not by a part of it.

Father's answer closes the discussion on that day. Nevertheless, that conversation sparks off other conversations in the homes of those parishioners and among the leaders and other groups. They all feel they would be ready for such a step if the whole Church would find it appropriate. They are united on one thing – they would welcome it with joyful hearts.

Is Silungile parish really ready?

Silungile parish feels ready. It is quite understandable that the parishioners feel that they are ready to implement such a new legislation of the Church, which would allow local voluntary leaders to be ordained as priests. They have several candidates whom everybody would certify as suitable and whom all would accept. They are convinced about the faith of these leaders, their life style, their knowledge and ability.

They certainly have no problems such as mentioned by the questioner in the above letter. There is no need for a preparatory phase of conscientization in the community or for initial training. These factors have been taken care of long ago. There is also no fear that they could not support ordained local leaders. Their leaders have never asked for any financial support and, if one were ordained, they are sure he would provide for himself and his family as he has always done.

They are ready. They foresee no problems. What about problems that might arise in the future? They have not spoken about that. They have not determined whether ordination would be limited to only *one* leader. The writer of the first letter above assumes that only one from the village would be ordained. Is it likely that the priests of Silungile would do the same and suggest that only *one* should be ordained in each village? If only *one*, what if he got into trouble? What if he committed a serious offence, an offence which could not be proved? If part of the community felt they could no longer receive the sacraments from him while others felt they had to defend their relative – how could such a dilemma be solved? This is only one theoretical problem, but there could be others of which they have no idea at the moment, problems which they have not considered in their initial sense that the ordination of one of their local leaders would be a possible solution.

They also have not considered the position of the two present priests with whom they get on so well at present. What would happen to this relationship if one of their own were ordained? Are they sure that their own local part-time priest would not try to imitate the two full-time ones? Would the sickness which some people call "clericalism" not infect their own man? Why should it? They do not think about that; they think only of solving the problem of the rare opportunities for the Eucharist and other sacraments. They believe that they just have to wait for the lawmakers' decision. Are the lawmakers preparing to make the decision?

The city parish of Ovestown is weary of "borrowing" priests

The parish is near the airport, quite a noisy place to live. Even on Sundays the priest often has to pause when the noise of the planes taking off is too overpowering. The noise problem has lessened since the new air-conditioning was installed in the parish Church; they can now keep the windows closed. It was quite costly but they managed easily because most of the parishioners are well off and can afford to support their Church.

The airport noise is, however, not the worst problem of the small parish on the outskirts of the city. A far more serious one is the shortage of priests. The parish council has to phone around each week to find a priest for the next Sunday. They have become fed up with this continual search for a priest that they can get hold of for an hour. In the good old days the bishop had many priests and their small elite parish had its own priest. But for quite some time things have been changing in the diocese.

They no longer have a priest of their own. The priest who should actually care for them has to serve four parishes, and the other three parishes are much larger than Ovestown.

The overburdening of the one priest who has to serve four parishes has resulted in their having been asked to conduct a Service of the Word twice a month, and it is this they do not like at all. They try to avoid it by phoning around to enquire whether there is perhaps a priest in one of the diocesan offices who can come on the Sunday when they are supposed to conduct their own service. Nobody likes this state of affairs. There are many highly educated people in the parish, but to stand in front of the others and conduct a service? No. They have not been prepared for this.

Some of the parishioners recently attended a very interesting lecture in the Catholic University. The lecturer spoke of the need to re-think the whole question of ministry and priesthood, and he also mentioned the possibility that in places where there are great shortages of priests a local proven person could be ordained priest to work on a part-time basis. This idea has since been discussed with other members of the parish. Of course, they could find somebody to attend evening courses at the Catholic University and train as a part-time priest. Then the problem of the "priestless" services on Sundays would be solved once and for all.

Many questions arise from the Story of Ovestown

A very different parish, a very different social milieu, and yet the solution would appear to be the same as for other parishes. Really? Are there not too many obstacles in Ovestown parish to even remotely consider solving the problem by this method? Can a local proven Christian be ordained priest before the community is properly prepared to accept the changed method of ministry? As the parish is described, it is obvious that it is dangerously passive and has hardly undertaken any steps towards community building. How will an ordained "proven" person fit into such a passive congregation? How will that person be accepted?

It is quite likely that the parishioners are thinking in terms of only *one* of them being ordained, which means that he will be expected to be available all the time. The others will retain their rather passive attitude and rely on this one ordained person to do everything for them, Sunday after Sunday and also often during the week. Will such a person not feel uncomfortable in such an exposed position? Will he not be overburdened? If so, will it not be suggested from all sides that he should rather become a full-time priest? A suitable salary is no problem in a well-to-do parish of this kind.

A settlement of this kind would make them all the happier and leave them free to retain their passive stance. Any attempt to lead the parish to a community vision of Church would then be difficult.

Are there perhaps still other issues which should be considered before this solution is proposed?

"If Father Masifunde's parish remains an exception, we cannot ordain"

"Masifunde" is his local nickname. In English it means "Let us learn." He got the name from his insistent emphasis on encouraging the training of leaders. He keeps on reminding each group of leaders in his area that there is more and more to learn and that there is no end to formation and training.

His efforts have borne fruit. When you go to his parish you can see the result. There are trained parish councils in each of the fifteen widely scattered communities he serves. There are trained leaders for the many parish activities: small faith-sharing groups, marriage enrichment groups, the Service of the Word when there is no priest, and for funerals. There are even trained leaders for those tasks which are often overlooked in parishes, such as Justice & Peace and Development.

On-going training for all the leaders takes place yearly. Mostly it is Father Masifunde himself who conducts the sessions. Where more specialized instruction is required Father invites professionals. The training is never technically, academically orientated but always community-related. All training has a community dimension. Nobody is "trained away" from the community but is rather, through the formation s/he receives, brought nearer to the community.

One day Father Masifunde became part of a heated discussion between the Vicar General and Father Hlala. Father Hlala complained that in their diocese people never discussed possible ways of overcoming the shortage of priests: "Do you not read? Don't you realize that one day we will have to ordain local proven leaders? Why don't you press ahead?"

"Do you think the Pope would agree if we were to ask for permission to ordain local leaders?" asked the Vicar General.

"Of course he will not agree unless all dioceses make a united appeal and persist in demanding it."

"That would be difficult. But tell me, are we ourselves ready to make such a request? I do not think we are. The majority is not prepared for so vast a change."

"What do you mean by 'ready'? Do you think that we have no suitable candidates for ordination? You are mistaken. In my parish I can immediately point out an excellent lay leader, and in each of our parishes I am sure we can find one," replied Father Hlala in an almost angry tone.

The Vicar General remained calm: "No. In questioning our readiness I was not referring to any problem about finding a good candidate. I know our parishes and I am sure we could find such a person in each of them. What I fear is that we are not ready to give such people the continuous, ongoing formation they would require. If we were to ordain them and then leave them to function alone, that would lead to disaster..."

He paused a moment, then pointed to Father Masifunde who was observing their dispute in silence. "This is what I mean by being 'ready,' what he has been doing. All his leaders have been trained and, what is more, are always open to receiving more training to improve their leadership qualities for the good of the community. In his parish I would not be afraid that any leader would refuse training and tell me: 'I know enough, leave me alone.' Ongoing formation is a reality there. Were we to ordain local leaders in Father Masifunde's parish we could rest assured that things would not go wrong."

Father Masifunde tried to play down this lavish praise from his Vicar General: "Well, I do not think we are such an exception in our parish. There are a few other parishes of the diocese who are doing the same, but by far, not all, I admit."

The Vicar General took that up: "By far not all, that is very true. I would of course not wait until the very last parish had set out on that road of continuous training. But it would have to be the majority of parishes. Only then could we confidently say we are ready."

Is Father Masifunde's diocese an exception?

Probably not. Just as in his diocese only a minority of parishes is ready, so it is in many dioceses and so in the whole Church. There are parts of the Church which are actually ready, or almost ready, for the day when the decision to ordain local proven leaders is made. The question we have to face is: Which are more numerous, the parishes of Father Masifunde or those of Father Hlala who is not even aware that there are preconditions to be fulfilled before we should ask for the permission to ordain proven leaders?

If we have to reply that the type of Father Masifunde's parish is the exception or in the minority, could we then press for the Universal Church to make this decision? Or would we first have to work hard to reach that stage of readiness in the great majority of our parishes?

There are not only parishes but whole dioceses of which one could say that they are more or less ready for such a step. If they were allowed to go ahead and ordain proven leaders in many of their parishes what about the effects this would have on neighbouring dioceses which are not ready?

Should we not pose the same question on the next level as well? What about whole countries? Are there countries of which we can say that the Church is more or less ready to introduce the ordination of local proven leaders? If the reply is that it is only a minority of countries which are ready, what effect would it have in other parts of the world if these "prepared" countries went ahead alone?

To return to the three priests and their conversation, how can other parishes be helped to adopt Father Masifunde's approach? How can the Vicar General convince his bishop and the other priests of his diocese that they should not hammer the Pope to make the decision but rather prove that they are ready for it?

"Even the ordination of a pensioner will do"

Three elderly women stood chatting outside the Church where they had just finished their Sunday celebration. It had been a so-called "priestless" service, a Service of the Word.

"This is the second Sunday this month that we have had no priest, what a shame!" complained one of the women.

Another added: "How can this continue? Has the Bishop no idea how to get a priest for us?"

"What will happen to our Church? We are no longer doing things the Catholic way," added the third one shaking her head. "What do our grandchildren learn when they go to Church? What is Sunday for them? Won't they begin to think that Mass and the so-called Service of the Word are one and the same? They will not see that there is a difference."

After a short pause, the one who had started the conversation moved closer to the other two and spoke in a subdued tone: "I read an article in the last diocesan paper. It was about a group of priests overseas discussing whether the priest shortage could be alleviated by ordaining married men?"

"Really!" exclaimed the second woman. "If the married priest had a family, how could the Church afford to support such a person in every town?"

"No, no," continued the first, "they spoke of ordaining men who would do priestly work in their spare time. They would not work full-time. They would not be employed by the diocese."

"Not possible," objected the third woman. "How could anyone do a priest's work in his spare time? I can't see that working."

"Not so impossible," the main speaker continued, "look at Mr. Dala in our parish. He is always there when some help is needed. He is absolutely reliable. And we know him well. He has proved himself worthy over the years. And he has time now as he is pensioned."

"You are right," agreed the second, "he would be ideal. People like him have the time and, above all, they are old and will not easily change as young men might."

"Mr. Dala would be our choice for our town. For our neighbouring town I would know a like choice, also a pensioner. Actually I think we would find such a person in almost every place. I would stress that a pensioner is the answer because..."

The second woman interrupted her: "When you first mentioned the possibility of a married man being ordained a priest, I was rather shocked. We have grown up with the belief that a priest is celibate. I am still not quite at ease with the idea. What frightens me is the thought that he could have a problem in his marriage. Imagine the reaction that would cause, when parishioners hear about it and see him the next Sunday at the altar. That is why I like your suggestion of people like Mr. Dala. He is no longer young and we know that things have been sorted out in his marriage. We will not get surprises about him."

"I was going to say that a pensioner not only has the time but also that he doesn't have to spend his time worrying about his livelihood. You see Mr. Dala taking a walk every morning. He goes every day to look after his bees; he wants something to do with his time. And he is a man who loves his faith, so he would surely spend time on Church work. If ever a new kind of priest is introduced into the Church, people like him should be chosen."

The third woman added a human dimension to their serious discourse: "Another thing I like about a pensioner is that he is less likely to rail at us. Young people can become so heated about problems; they could even shout at us in Church. A pensioner would be more controlled. If we are to have married priests, then this is the way forward, pensioner priests."

As they walked away all three were in agreement, the most informed lady echoing the hope of the other two that the Church would ordain their choice of person and would do it soon.

You see no problems with pensioners?

This kind of conversation is typical of concerned people in various places over the last years. Many sincerely believe that the priest shortage could be solved in this way and they see no problems with it. Are there none?

It is true that this solution satisfies several important concerns: the ordained lay pensioner will have the time to work for the community; it will not mean any additional financial burden for the parish; parishioners can rest assured that their priest will live a good Christian life.

In our hypothetical story the women who favour this solution are elderly. What about other age groups? How would they feel about it? How would the youth of the community react to such a proposal?

It is understandable that the ordination of pensioners is widely seen as a solution, but the fact that it is so often suggested contains the danger that we would have too many pensioners in the presbyterium of the diocese. If they become the majority in the presbyteria, would they not sway the decision-making of the whole Church towards the view point of the elderly?

A great advantage in ordaining local proven leaders is that it would help to bring faith and life together. The mode of life of those officiating at the altar would not differ from that of the people in the pew. However, a situation where only pensioners are seen at the altar would distort the whole image of Church. Wouldn't the younger and more energetic members of the community feel uneasy? Wouldn't we be in danger of becoming a pensioner-Church?

Are we not perhaps making the mistake of looking at the problem of priest shortage from too constricted an angle, of seeing it only as a way to provide greater frequency of the sacraments? Could narrow-minded questions lead us to short-sighted solutions?

Mr. Diploma: "I am ready to be ordained"

The table in front of him was full of books. There was the lectionary and there was the full bible. On the side there was a Greek bible as well and a Greek dictionary, and there were two bible commentaries next to the computer. With his hands on the key board, Mr. Diploma had his eyes fixed on the monitor screen where the first part of the sermon for next Sunday began to take shape.

"Are you still busy?" whispered his wife as she quietly entered the office.

"Yes. You had better go on your own to the festival and take the children with you. I'll follow later."

He heard her leaving with her car. A half hour later he followed in his own car, still deeply pondering over the matter of the sermon he would deliver on Sunday.

Mr. Diploma lived in the presbytery of this relatively small parish. It was an old parish in a well-known historical town of Germany. Their magnificent church, too, was historic. They had a solidly-built and well-equipped parish presbytery, but they had no priest. Mr. Diploma was transferred to the parish by the bishop the previous year, after the parish councilors had repeatedly gone to the bishop requesting him to appoint a priest to their parish. Each time they went, it was with a bigger delegation, and each time they stated their case more forcibly. The bishop reiterated that he had no priest for them, that even larger parishes had to be served by neighbouring priests. But they kept on begging the bishop, on each successive occasion making the matter more urgent. The bishop, on his part, counteracted with new assertions of the increasing shortage of priests in the diocese.

In the end, the bishop said the only solution was to transfer one of the highly trained lay-theologians called "Pastoral Assistants" to their town. He could live in the presbytery. At least the empty presbytery building would no longer be a constant cause of anger among the people. Those who were used to going to the presbytery for a baptism certificate, or to request instruction before marriage, or to report a death and ask for a funeral service – all those would no longer find a closed door. They would know that the Pastoral Assistant was there and he would help them as far as a non-ordained person could. On the Sundays when no priest could go to the parish, he would take the service and give a well prepared sermon. He would conduct all funerals and give catechetical instruction. Many of the people's needs would be fulfilled even if they no longer had a priest.

Mr. Diploma had no financial difficulties. He received a good salary from the diocese, on the level of other professionals with a full university diploma. He had finished his six years of theological studies at the university and had no reason to feel inferior to any of the priests. In fact he felt even more up to date theologically than many of them.

Nevertheless he had misgivings which he would, on occasion, confide to his wife: "You know, I felt so awkward yesterday. I completed the preparation for the marriage of a couple and then they asked me when I could conduct their marriage service. I had to reply that I could not do that because I am not a priest. They said that, in their view, I prepared them better than any priest could have done. When the bride-to-be suggested they ask the bishop to make me a priest, I explained very briefly the Church law about ordination. I could see that they did not know much about it and that they were beginning to feel resentful towards the Church hierarchy. I had to try to calm them down. Yet I felt I was convincing neither them nor myself. I am a fully qualified theologian. I live in the parish house, but I am not what I should be."

"This is not the first time you talk like this," his wife replied sympathetically, "and I agree with you. Why doesn't the Church listen to the people? You told me that the members of the diocesan synod were unanimous in their appeal to the bishop to beg Rome to allow the ordination of married *viri probati*. He may be right in thinking that Rome might not agree, but how can he say that he also sees problems? What problems does he see? There are no problems. The candidates are ready. Here you are."

"It is not that I am proud of my qualifications or that I am insisting it should be qualified people like me, but yes, it's true that we Pastoral Assistants are ready."

Questions to Mr. Diploma and his superiors

About Mr. Diploma's readiness there are probably no questions, least of all about his theological ability. About his personal dedication, his lifestyle, his spirituality we have few doubts. It is the contrast between the situation of Mr. Diploma in the above type of parish and the very different situation in some of the other stories that gives rise to questions. Those concerned all ask for a like solution, the permission to ordain married proven leaders, but the backgrounds from which they make their request are vastly different. Although all are united in their desire for a similar solution, there is a striking dissimilarity between the active communities which bring forth their own leaders and the passive congregations who want to be cared for. So, while their intent is the same – to overcome the shortage of priests by introducing a new kind of priest – their whole mode of living the faith is at odds.

If the solution they are asking for were granted, would it not result in disparate implementations? Are the people of the two very different situations and their bishops and priests aware that their requests, though apparently the same, are in fact not so? Do they not perceive that they are asking for something before first discerning the consequences? Do they not act like the passengers in an airplane demanding it should take off before the pilot knows where there is a place to land?

Mr. Diploma considers himself the only candidate in the town. But if this parish were to become an active community by encouraging many of its members to become involved in Church work and to undergo training, there would be many suitable candidates. Wouldn't it be better for the community if a team of locally-born leaders were to be ordained instead of one who comes from somewhere else and needs a high salary? And wouldn't the ordination of Mr. Diploma serve to perpetuate the deplorable passivity of the Catholics of this town? Once he is ordained they would surely opt to continue as they always have done. Yet this is not what he himself wants to see.

There was no serious reflection on the part of the parishioners before they began pestering the bishop to give them a priest, or when the bishop agreed to place the Pastoral Assistant in their empty presbytery. Likewise when the desire to have him ordained originated with the engaged couple, there was no discernment of the consequences to the parishioners.

Wouldn't it be essential for concerned people and their pastors belonging to the various types of communities to get to know the multiplicity of situations in which the same solution is being proposed? And wouldn't it be fundamental to the whole issue for them somehow to reflect together on the many consequences such a step would generate?

Bishop Futura prays for more priests

"Lord, be with the priests of my diocese, with all two hundred of them, with each one of them. You know they are overburdened. You know they are too few.

"Lord, call many young men to be priests so that the many thousands of the faithful will receive the sacraments. I do not know why you allow vocations to be so few. I do not know what in your wisdom you have in mind for us.

"You know that our parishes no longer have the Eucharist every Sunday, yet surely it is your wish for them to have it. We observe how the parishioners gradually get used to this and even think it normal. We notice that they lose the sense of the sacraments, but what can we do, we whom you called to be responsible pastors of the diocese and of the whole Church?"

Bishop Futura has been bishop for fifteen years. When he kneels at night in his small chapel he feels inadequate for the task of governing his diocese. He knows what he should be doing but he feels unable to do it. It is the nagging consciousness of so many of his parishes without a priest that causes him the most anxiety. So he keeps on praying for some kind of enlightenment:

"Lord, what shall I say when my people ask me to send a request to Rome for the ordination of married proven leaders? Is it the right request? Can I truly say I support it? Will it be a step forward or a step in the wrong direction? Once that move is made it cannot be undone; it will be either right or wrong for ever. Help us to see whether it is right."

"Lord, enlighten the Pope to make this decision for us and let it be the right decision, not the wrong one. But no, I should not leave things to him as if he were the only one to decide. I know I should decide with him. I know I should act as his brother. I know that I and my fellow bishops should present clearly reflected proposals to him. I know it is all of us who have to carefully prepare the decision, but we have no clarity about it."

"Lord, help us to foresee what will happen if we were to allow the ordination of local proven leaders. Will the present priests feel supported or discouraged by the change in their way of life? Will they be strengthened or will they lose their dedication? Will it help the people's faith to grow or will it bring chaos into the Church? In the past everybody knew who was a priest and who not, but if hundreds or thousands of this new kind of priest were to appear, would we and the people not get confused?

"If even in the present situation where priests are celibate and full time, it is difficult to keep all of them on the right path and to unify them somehow, will this not become impossible with priests whom the bishop hardly knows, who are at their work place most of the day, who have no time to come to meetings, who are occupied with their families, who are financially totally independent, and in whose selection we bishops would have very little say?"

"Lord, we should know – and we do not know. We will do anything that is right even if it is difficult, but what is right? Of course we want more priests. Should we continue to look for them in the traditional way when that method seems to us to be no longer adequate? Or are you telling us that there is also a new way of fulfilling the needs of your growing Church? Lord help us to see what you want us to do."

What would you tell your bishop?

Bishops receive advice from many people. Sometimes it is unanimous advice, at other times it is quite contradictory. A careful scrutiny of the various suggestions made gives the impression that most of the advice offered is of a "short-cut" nature. It often indicates a desired result but does not give any idea of how it is to be achieved. In other instances it presents a decision the bishop should make, but not the careful weighing of arguments that have led to the proposal. Frequently the advice "do this" or "don't do that" is based on personal feeling, not on a careful analysis of the pros and cons. No wonder none of it has been taken up.

It is, however, probably more true to say that most bishops have not yet received any advice. But then have they asked for it? Probably most bishops do have an opinion for or against ordaining married proven local leaders but not a final one. The majority would be prepared to re-examine their reasoning, especially if there were someone to assist them.

This publication wants to do just that.

Father "Plenty" is shocked by Father "Share"

The World Eucharistic Congress had ended and the participants were preparing to return home. Some had made new friends and were sitting together in the lounge of the hotel. Two priests chatted over their final drink. Father Plenty and Father Share came from two very different countries.

"Father Plenty, you seem to be in a great hurry to leave," remarked Father Share.

"Yes, I have to fly tonight, the whole night through. I have to be home tomorrow in time for a funeral in my parish."

"But surely it can be conducted by somebody else?"

"No. The deceased was an important elderly lady. I am the only priest in the parish and in our parish it would be quite a sad thing for the family and the community if they had to ask another priest to bury her."

"A priest? Why not a lay leader? I, too, am the only priest. There is no way I could give the time for the hundreds of funeral services that take place annually in the parish. I have not presided over a funeral for the last ten years. All the funeral services are conducted by lay leaders."

"How big is your parish?"

"Seventy thousand Catholics."

"What? Seventy thousand! Incredible!" Father Plenty could not believe what he had heard. "My parish has seven hundred Catholics, and it is not the smallest in the diocese. What a difference! How can one priest serve seventy thousand?"

"Well, it is only possible because I work with hundreds of lay leaders."

Father Plenty wanted to know more: "What kind of lay leaders?"

"There are eleven large Base Communities, each with a church building and with a leadership team of plus/minus twelve men and twelve women. The last parish statistics numbered a total of 250 leaders. Some are authorized to baptise, others to solemnize marriages. There are liturgy leaders and funeral leaders. And this number doesn't include the catechism teachers of the various age groups. That would make another two hundred for the parish. Of course, all of them are voluntary workers."

"That amount of voluntary work is fantastic. We could never achieve that in our parishes. But what about Sunday Mass in those eleven churches?"

"That is our one great deficiency, for which we as a parish or within the diocese cannot yet provide a solution."

"So you live in one of those areas about which we read in our Church papers, where the shortage of priests is incredibly high. Tell me, was it not in such areas that the idea of ordaining lay leaders originated?"

"Yes, the proposal continues to be discussed. We pray and hope that it will soon become a reality."

Father Plenty remembered one of the reasons he had read against that idea and so he put it to his confrere: "It has been suggested that the ordination of lay leaders would clericalize the laity. Would there not be a danger that it might destroy the beautiful involvement of the laity you have built up in your parish?"

"If we would ordain one person for each church, yes. But we would carefully avoid that and we would ordain only several of the leaders who would then form a team in each of the communities. They would not dress like a priest; they would not be called 'Father'; they would take turns in functioning and this would ensure their continuing to live like their co-parishioners. In this way we would greatly reduce the danger that clericalization could develop."

"I must say I envy you for that amount of lay involvement. It makes people feel they are the Church. I suppose we could only achieve it in our diocese if we were fewer priests. Look at me. I must fly home to-night to conduct a funeral, because I am the Church in my area. You have many more people to be concerned about and yet you can afford to fly tomorrow because your people know they are the Church. I'm getting confused. We believe we need more priests to care for the people; but if we have sufficient priests how will we ever become a Church which is a community?"

"I think the idea of the priest as the one who 'cares' for the people must disappear or must be transformed in one way or another, whether through a shortage of priests or in another way. What are you doing in your country to achieve that? Is the ordination of lay leaders not also being discussed in your country?"

"Out of the question. It would be considered a crazy idea. Even the smallest parish has its priest, so there is no problem about any shortage. Nobody would understand why any of our bishops would want to ordain *viri probati*. We, too, have excellent lay people, though they have little function in the life of the Church. If one of them were to be ordained a priest, he would be looked on as a queer kind of half-cleric. The ordination of lay leaders would serve no purpose and would undermine the existing priesthood. Such an innovation would damage the Church in our country irreparably. Our bishops would oppose the proposal very forcefully."

"I can see a dilemma. If your bishops succeed in blocking the ordination of local leaders in the Church, the Church in my country and many other areas will be adversely affected. If our bishops prevail, it will be detrimental for the Church in your part of the world. It seems we have to look for a solution that will be satisfactory to the Church as a whole. I hope that can be reached."

Father Plenty pondered in silence for a while. Then he had another question: "If the bishops do come to some kind of agreement, would all priests accept the new dispensation? Even in areas where the shortage of priests prevents regular reception of the sacraments, will all the priests be as open-minded as you are? Won't many feel threatened by the enormous change?"

"Not too many," Father Share felt, "but we still have to do a lot of reflection."

There was a most cordial parting between the two churchmen as Father Plenty hurried off to get to the airport.

Father Somnia – between nightmares and hopes

Father Somnia usually sleeps well, but tonight he has been lying awake for a long time and many thoughts are going through his mind. During the day he had a long discussion with another priest. They spoke about the shortage of priests and what could be done to alleviate it. As can be expected, the possibility of permission one day being granted to ordain local leaders occupied most of the conversation.

What he contributed to their dialogue and the responses and ideas of his friend now keep rising to the surface of his consciousness. He begins to fantasize what it would be like should the permission be given.

In every town there will be dozens of part-time priests. Every outstation, every village will have a few who can celebrate the Eucharist. In large Church meetings there will be the bishop, a handful of full-time priests and a hundred part-time priests. There will be some difficulty in knowing who is who. What is the one over there? and the one on the other side? Is he a full-time priest or is he an ordained lay leader?

How will I fit into those changed circumstances? Everybody knows who I am now, the only priest far and wide. But then, the word "priest" will be nothing special because there will be so many priests – the busdriver, the bank teller, the postmaster, the butcher.... Who exactly will I be then? As parish priest in the present system, I am often called to an outstation to settle conflicts. There is no one else who can do it except me, the people's priest. In the possible new Church structure, when there would be various "priests" to call on, I foresee a lot of confusion.

Conflicts arise from time to time in various parts of my parish; sometimes it is a dispute about leadership. The people concerned cannot settle it among themselves. I meet with them and listen to their views. We discuss the matter at length according to the seriousness of the problem. We can usually come to a cordial decision that satisfies all parties but only because I, the priest, am present. The people would not, and probably are not able to, settle it on their own. I wonder how it would work out should there be several priests among the local leaders, with relatives on various sides? That could be a nightmare – chaos, a split in the Church or something equally devastating."

When people cannot sleep, many ideas are tossed around, and the mood of their mind fluctuates. After that string of doubts and fears, Fr Somnia's thoughts became more positive. He remembered a time when he had been similarly plagued by apprehension. It was when the lay ministries were introduced. He feared then that he would lose his control over the parish. If funerals were conducted by many lay leaders and not by himself, would he lose his identity? That fear soon proved unfounded. Since then he has assumed a new role among the many leaders and is happy with it, very happy actually. Couldn't the same happen again? He knows the good will of the people. He can depend on the continuity of their love for him as pastor, not just because he is presently the only one to celebrate the Eucharist, but also because he is a spiritual friend and in a sense a unique leader. The newly-created leaders were trained by him and they remain eager to have him at their side. The hope that he could experience the same transition in a possible new dispensation lulls him off to sleep.

* * *

Let us end our stories here. Hundreds more could be added. They are all real in the sense that all the situations exist; these fears and hopes can be observed everywhere. The short stories serve to remind us that it is not only one situation or one attitude which forms the background to the question of the ordination of *viri probati*. Too often we notice that those who argue for or against are basing their opinion on only one situation. The reality is more complex.

In order to understand each other's situation and the each other's proposals let us now try to list several main categories of situations from which the call for *viri probati* ordinations is emanating or could emanate.

The main categories among those situations

Passive congregations cared for by a priest-substitute

The loudest calls for the ordination of *viri probati* probably come from those who are actually not the ones most in need. They come from parishes in parts of Europe and North America where the number of priests has declined drastically over the past decades. The reactions of those areas to the shortage of priests depended on the financial situation of the Church in the region. The countries where the Church is financially well off because it can rely on a Church tax collected by the government have introduced employed pastoral workers to fulfil many tasks which were previously performed by the priests. In some areas they are called "pastoral assistants" and they gradually became a kind of substitute for the missing priests in those areas. Other countries relied more on deacons who were voluntary workers, and in again other countries pastoral teams tried to make up for the shortage of priests.

In Mission countries there was a shortage of priests centuries ago and solutions had to be found. Substitutes for the missing priests were introduced in the form of employed lay pastors, called "catechists". Statistics of catechists showed, in the peak time of the 1960's, a number as high as 108 000 for all continents but mainly in the areas of the Young Churches, and the majority of these were substitutes for the missing priests. Only a smaller percentage of this high number were catechism teachers and catechetical workers. Among the majority of the lay pastor "catechists", some were voluntary leaders while others were fully employed or partly employed by the Church. The peak time of catechists as lay pastors may be over, but in the Young Churches many large parishes are still structured on some form of this combination of too few priests and a good number of substitutes, called "catechists".

Where there are priest substitutes over a long period of time, the question must arise whether these could not be transformed into the real thing. It is therefore not surprising that suggestions were made several times that the pastoral assistants, or the deacons, or the catechists – at least some of them – should be ordained priests.

As we, in this opening part, briefly describe the different situations from which the call for the ordination of viri probati is arising, we should also realize that in all situations where a substitute for the missing priests already exists, the call for viri probati priests takes on a special character. The search for possible candidates for viri probati ordinations must automatically focus on the existing substitute. We will examine later whether the choice of these substitutes would really be a good solution. We will also have to ask ourselves what kind of Church would be created if these substitutes were ordained. On the other hand, if some of us would prefer to ordain not these substitutes but others, the problem would arise how to bypass the obvious candidates. All these questions and problems are caused by the one rather widespread fact that these substitutes do exist.

Passive congregations which look for any kind of provider

There are parishes which suffer in a similar way from the shortage of priests but, in contrast to the above examples, do not have a clearly defined substitute. They might accept any substitute but they do not get one. The few remaining priests are serving three or more parishes as well as they can, but many pastoral tasks just remain unfulfilled. On many Sundays there is simply no service at all in the parish church, and those who can and are sufficiently motivated use their vehicles to attend Mass in a neighbouring parish.

These parishes are usually of the old traditional type, and the faithful miss the care the priests have always provided. They want Sunday Mass, funerals, baptisms and marriages to be provided for them. They continue to complain to the bishop and ask for a priest but they cannot get one.

Since there is no officially established substitute for the priest, there will be some attempts to find another kind of provider. It may be a person who leads the rosary or an exceptional person who celebrates a Service of the Word on Sundays. In some cases it could be a pensioner who conducts funerals. People who can fulfil many of these pastoral tasks would exist in most places but in the public eye their work might not be acceptable.

In many situations of this kind, especially in First World countries, nobody tries to make a start with community building which would enable the parish to become aware that it holds the key to the solution. There are many convinced and committed Catholics among them and there are many who have the time and the talents to work voluntarily for the community, but there is nobody to initiate the process.

Situations of this second type would be found where the Church is financially not so well off and the hierarchy has therefore not been able to employ some kind of substitutes for the dwindling number of priests. At the same time the shortage of priests has not led to efforts to use this emergency in order to rethink the whole situation of these parishes.

Who is it who would call for the ordination of *viri probati* priests in this kind of diocese? Is it the bishop or the priests? Is it the few Catholics who read theological books? Whoever it may be, the one thing that is clear about those parishes and that diocese is that there is no real basis for this request. There is no ground work on which the request could be based. It comes out of a vacuum and this is certainly dangerous. Of course there are good proven Catholics in these parishes, just as many as elsewhere. What is missing is awareness raising, community building and ministry training. The Catholics have not yet realized that they themselves are the Church. They do not yet see it as a value that some of their own ranks fulfil tasks for the community. In the beginning stages they might reject being served by somebody who comes from among themselves and is like themselves. It takes some time and certain processes before they see this as a value. If anybody were to bypass this stage of growth and immediately begin the search for candidates for ordination among the proven members of the congregation, this would lead rather to more tensions and more dissatisfaction.

Members of this kind of parish are certainly not ready for the introduction of *viri probati* priests. Neither are their priests ready, judging from the way their parishes live their faith. Even if *viri probati* priests were ordained in this situation, the existing few priests would not know how to relate to them. The only thing that cries for the ordination of additional priests in this case is the empty altar, nothing else. There is another cry, an inaudible one, coming out of this situation, the cry for community building. Is it not true that Church leaders should realize it is essential to listen to the second before the first cry?

Passive congregations served by a pastoral team

In other parts of the Older Churches, the shortage of priests has also become severe and a low Church income has prevented the employment of highly paid substitutes for the lacking priests. Instead, the dioceses have put their minds together and have looked for other solutions. Several neighbouring parishes which no longer have priests are grouped together into a cluster parish. In some areas they have officially been formed into one large parish consisting of several congregations. In other areas the official parish structure has been left intact, but the administration is combined into one single service structure. In both cases it is this central administration and central animation which tries to solve the problem.

This central structure is often formed as a team consisting of one priest and a number of highly motivated lay people. Where possible a small group of religious Sisters is included in the central ministry team. These teams are known as "pastoral teams" or "equipes" or are called by some other term.

The pastoral team may serve three, four or even ten former parishes. It will do for them as much as it can do, and it usually has the intention of not doing all the work by itself. The team will rather try to form small work groups or local teams in each of the former parishes. The success of this effort varies greatly, according to the willingness of the faithful to move away from the former attitude of passively waiting to be served.

It is this latter aspect which in many cases limits the success of these efforts. The people have been quiescent for so long. For centuries they have been expected to accept passively the service of the priests. It requires great effort and great skill to lead people out of this deeply ingrained attitude. Consequently this praiseworthy effort often reaches no further than the parallel existence of a small and exemplary pastoral team with large passive congregations.

The call for the ordination of some proven local leaders will of course easily arise from such teams and even from their parishioners. If lay members of such pastoral teams were ordained what would it mean? It would have implications which are to some extent different from those situations we mentioned before. We will have to reflect on these implications later on.

We have described several types of passive congregations and noted that in many of them the call for the ordination of *viri probati* priests is voiced very forcefully. Is that demand not somehow suspect? Is it not true that many congregations of this kind and their priests and bishops actually want to use the new kind of priest to perpetuate the old vision of Church?

Active communities which became inaccessible to priests

We read many reports about the younger Churches in war-torn areas where parishes which were once lively communities became cut off from the priests and from the diocese for several years. Heart-rending stories are told of those communities and of their suffering. They endure incredible hardships because of war and on top of that are deprived of the sacramental life of the Church for long periods of time, sometimes for several years.

In contrast to the other situations described above, we often hear how these Christian communities continue to meet on their own to pray, to read the scriptures, to assist each other, and even to solemnize baptisms and marriages without a priest. They usually invent their own ministry structures or simply enlarge the existing forms of lay leadership. We read of voluntary catechists who act as community leaders or of other types of community leaders who emerge from among the people and cooperate with them.

Stories of this kind often end with questioning the fact why the Church does not provide a kind of priesthood which could function in such circumstances. It is evident that those communities would easily produce their own leaders among whom a number, if ordained priest, would be fully accepted by the community. They would not need full theological training nor would they need any financial support. Why our Church is not prepared for contingencies of this nature is the accusing question posed in such reports. It is known that the Church has actually done this in some cases but only as a rare exception surrounded by many questions and fears.

Stories of this kind are usually short and do not continue with careful reflection. What would happen if leaders were ordained just before such

crisis situations or during such times of need? What are the implications?
And is it not better to concentrate rather on the times and places where
there is not yet any crisis?

Where all communities are active and ready

There are thousands of parishes and communities which are not in a
crisis situation and yet lead a community life just as active and reliable as
those whom we admired during war times. They do exist.

Among the Younger Churches there are many dioceses where not just
the exceptional parish but practically every parish consists of active communities. The parish usually comprises ten to twenty Sunday-service communities, each having its simple Church building, each with its team of leaders.

The leaders have been trained over several years to conduct a Service
of the Word on Sundays where they take turns to give the homily. Each
local team of leaders has a few who are authorised to distribute communion to the congregation on Sunday and to the sick. A number are trained
as funeral leaders. Baptisms are so many that several members of the
team are trained and authorised to baptise infants and there are also some
who are appointed to solemnize marriages. Each community has its own
community council which usually has to meet without the priest. A few
times a year all community councils meet as the parish council.

"Training" is a well-known concept in those parishes. The parishioners frequently speak of training because there is a continual sequence of
training events for all kinds of leaders. Most training sessions take place
in the little church halls attached to the community centres within the
parish confines. Only the more complex training sessions are conducted in
a neighbouring parish or in the diocesan centre. No leader assumes that
his training is complete. The notion of ongoing, unending training is already a fixed tradition.

It is clear who are the trainers. It is mainly the one or two priests of
the large parish, but also some religious Sisters who serve the cluster-
parish. Only in rare cases is it possible to obtain the help of an expert who
would come to the parish to offer additional training. The priests of this

kind of parish have assumed a new role, that of the animator priest. In many dioceses one can say that not only the few outstanding priests but practically every priest has assumed this new role.

Parishes such as these are often very large – fifty to seventy thousand Catholics living in a compact area of several square miles on the outskirts of large cities or as widely scattered communities in an area of hundreds of square miles. The parish consists of ten to twenty communities, each with its own teams of leaders, so that the whole parish may have as many as two or even three hundred trained leaders. Sometimes only one priest serves such a parish, sometimes two. It is clear that the priest himself will never lead a funeral service because these are all administered by the lay leaders. Most of the infant baptisms and even marriages are conducted by the trained and authorised lay leaders.

When one visits this kind of parish one hears the parishioners talking a lot about their concerns but one does not notice any strident request for the ordination of their leaders. What a contrast to the passive congregations of the Older Churches who are vociferous in their demand for this innovation although their deprivations are much less!

It is this kind of active parish (and diocese) that one dares to say is ready for the permission to ordain local proven leaders. The communities are ready. They would joyfully accept the new kind of priest and would support them in every way, as they have cooperated well with their lay leaders for many years. The possible candidates are also ready. They have voluntarily spent the greater part of their free time on Church work. From the practical point of view, ordination would change hardly anything in their life and their work. They have emerged as key leaders because they have given proof of reliability. The priests, too, are ready. They would accept the key leaders if these were ordained. They would continue to assist them and to train them. They feel sure they would not become redundant if some leaders were ordained and they would therefore continue in their work as before. There is ample reason to say these parishes and dioceses would be ready.

In some countries these dioceses are the majority but, compared to the whole Church, they are a small exception. It is not the whole Church which is ready, only some parts of the Church.

Together with this kind of diocese we should mention others which are not quite ready but could be ready fairly soon. We mean dioceses which know the processes and have started them. They have moved a certain stretch on the path of community building. If they were told to get ready for the ordination of some of the community leaders they would know what to do and would be confident to achieve it within a few years.

Where active communities are like stars in an empty sky

We can find active and lively communities in practically all countries and in all dioceses. The trouble is that they often exist as a rare exception within a diocese. We can read of these exceptional parishes in many publications, and there are many others which one discovers only by chance. They do exist almost everywhere. In most of the Older Churches we find these parishes among the great majority of passive ones.

Parishes of this kind are usually the fruit of the work of one charismatic priest. They are not the result of diocesan planning nor the result of a special need of that particular place. The existence of this type of parish almost everywhere might serve as an indication that in most situations something of this kind would be possible.

We find in these parishes a wide sharing of tasks and a large number of ministries. The leaders work in teams. We usually see a process in which many people take part and to which many can contribute their ideas. This gives rise to the emergence of many charisms and talents and provides the opportunity for people to learn a lot together.

It is in situations of this kind that a request for the ordination of some of the leaders deserves attention. This is natural because in these parishes it becomes clear that there is always a much greater reservoir of charisms than one might think. Among the people who possess the charisms are those who could very well be entrusted with the role of the ordained. Why not ordain those who have proven this beyond doubt?

We also observe that in parishes of the above calibre there has been no detailed follow-up to a suggestion to ordain leaders. No one has reflected on how the neighbouring parishes would be affected by such a move. No one has considered what would happen if that enlightened priest would one day leave his parish and a priest of a different mind take over. Is it not clear that a diocese and a whole country could not risk taking this step as long as these parishes remain an exception? Granted, one cannot wait until all parishes have introduced community building. What kind of majority or what percentage does one need before one dare ordain local leaders? If it is dangerous for a single parish to go it alone, to what extent does the same apply to neighbouring countries? It again reminds us that we cannot look only at our own situation but must also consider those of our neighbouring areas.

Where community building is favoured, but only up to a point

There is another kind of situation in many dioceses and countries. It is the one where community building has been successful but has not gone beyond a certain level. Things are done together. Leaders exist, but they are still quite dependent. They still leave too many decisions to the priest. In some parishes it is more the priest who seems to set limits to responsibilities and to the level of training. In other parishes one has the impression that the boundary is fixed by the leaders who want to shoulder responsibility only up to a certain point. It is not easy to pinpoint exactly who sets a limit to the process. The result, however, is clear. It is that leaders remain on the level of helpers and cannot yet be considered to be co-responsible leaders. The will to move on to real sharing is not yet there.

Training exists in these parishes but it is contained. It has not yet dawned on either the priest or the leaders that training and formation go from one horizon to the next. Or is there a certain fear that a distance must remain? Is there perhaps a hidden conviction that the levels of clerical and lay leadership should not become too close to each other?

In some parts of the world, especially in the Younger Churches, we find many of these parishes. What does their existence say to us? Is there perhaps a connection between this phenomenon and the refusal of their clergy to consider any form of ordination of local leaders? Why did they refuse to introduce the permanent diaconate? We were not given the exact reasons for the refusal to even discuss the ordination to the permanent diaconate in those areas. Those priests may have many reasons but is this insistence on keeping others at a lower level perhaps also one of them? It is certainly significant that most of them were sure that the communities should not even be informed that such a possibility exists and still less that it should be discussed with the people. We can imagine that something similar would happen if the Church would begin to discuss the possibility of ordaining *viri probati* priests.

We have too often heard the allegation that people have not been given more training because they did not want it or because they were unable to receive more training. It is not easy to prove the reasons for these claims. We just hope that there is no unconscious desire to limit the growth of co-responsibility.

It remains a fact that this situation exists. It will have an important impact on the question: In which parts of the universal Church it is feasible to ordain local proven leaders as *viri probati* priests?

Where participation is still a silent cry

There are still areas where every parish has its priest, where there is Mass every Sunday, where every infant is baptized and every deceased Christian solemnly buried by the priest. There is no need for more priests in those areas. These situations exist in the Church, even today.

What if these parishes hear of areas of the Church where the ordination of local lay leaders is envisaged? What if they would not only hear about the idea but would also be told that it is legally possible as from a certain date?

Surely there is no scarcity of sacraments in these areas. If, as we have seen above, the scarcity of the sacraments is usually taken as the only motive for the ordination of local leaders, then to speak about it in dioceses where there are sufficient priests is obviously meaningless.

It will even be considered destructive to the faith in those areas to speak of this kind of ordination because it seems to lower the high status of the present priests. It could sow doubts in their minds and endanger their commitment. Just the mere mention of it might cause confusion. Whereas in the past it was taken for granted that priesthood in the Catholic Church meant one clearly defined form and nothing else, the very idea of *viri probati* could destroy this clarity.

We have not yet studied those situations fully. We see that it apparently makes no sense to speak of the ordination of proven Christians in such circumstances. However, we have not yet looked deeper into the unconscious or unspoken aspirations of the Christians of those parishes. Are we sure they are so different from the active Christians in other parts of the world that we have considered? Perhaps they would not choose their kind of passive Church life if they knew it could be different and if they had the freedom to choose. It could be that they are unconsciously eager to share in all forms of Christian life but have never learned that such sharing is possible? Probably there is, deep down and very hidden, an aspiration towards co-responsibility and participation which is just as strong as in the active communities of other continents. If this is so – and it is quite likely – how should those in power respond to it?

However true this may be, it is also true that other sections of the Church where it is imperative to raise the question of *viri probati* priests at this time, have to be aware that there are large areas of the Church where any discussion of this theme will be openly disliked and rejected.

* * *

What does this brief look at the main situations tell us? It reminds us that the call for the ordination of local proven leaders comes from very different positions. It makes us aware that those who so urgently demand that this step be taken have different circumstances in mind. They are often only aware of certain situations and overlook others.

An analysis of the various conditions reveals that there is too narrow a concern with only one aspect, the infrequent celebration of the sacraments. Even those who live in areas where community building is the normal way of parish life, are taking it for granted and do not realize that our goal of community building should actually be a motive of its own for ordaining local leaders to lead the sacramental celebrations. They only ask for the ordination of local leaders when the sacraments become rare. It remains their only motive.

Parishes that have insufficient priests and are not geared towards community building will more naturally be concerned with the same one aspect and they, too, will have only one motive for finding an additional kind of priest. The whole debate about *viri probati* priests seems to suffer from this narrow focus on the scarcity of sacraments.

This narrow focus on sacraments is probably also the reason for there being hardly any concern for the future of the existing priests. People just want more priests because they need greater availability of the sacraments. They seem to have no time to consider what the ordination of a new kind of priest will mean for the present ones.

There are thousands of parishes where the existing priests have already assumed a new role as trainers, animators, unifiers and coordinators. Although publications abound which report that in large areas of the Church the present priests have already assumed a new role, we hear many voices in the Old Churches warning against creating two classes of priests. It will be our task in the following chapters to show that the fruitful interaction between these priests who are regional animators and the local leaders is already emerging. We will have to clarify that the creation of two classes of ordained leaders, one regional and the other local, is not a problem but is part of the solution. Whereas it seems to many that we need only one new kind of priest to replenish the shortage of the existing ones, we are beginning to see that we need two new kinds of priest.

The possible ordination of local leaders will be a change of enormous magnitude. It can not be discussed as a local issue but must be considered on world level. It will therefore be the duty of all to try to become aware of the different circumstances and the different patterns that form Church life in the various parts of the world. Those who demand that such a great step be taken have the duty to consider what it will imply in other parts of the Universal Church.

A further aspect of our present situation is that several attempts have already been made to move towards *viri probati* ordinations. It should be a warning to us that many of them were abandoned. We realize that this is not an easy field. The way people look at this question differs, and there is much confusion and contradiction. The following short chapter illustrates this.

Some tried to make a start but got stuck

The ensuing stories are all based on real events but some names of persons and countries have had to be changed because the incidents have not yet been published. The few anecdotes are typical examples of the much greater number of unsuccessful debates and attempts which have taken place. Other innovators have tried similar experiments or made comparable reflections. Let these stories serve as a reminder for us to be careful in dealing with this question.

"We see no problem at all. Let's just start"

A Canadian priest who taught theology at one of the seminaries in a Third World country met a missionary Sister who had in former times worked closely with him for several years. Greetings were exchanged and then Father shifted the conversation to the topic of the shortage of priests.

"Why does our Church still refuse to ordain proven lay leaders? There is no reason to continue postponing this step. It is the only answer to the shortage of priests."

"I am of the same opinion," replied Sister, "but are you sure we are ready for it?"

"Of course we are. In this country, though we are dealing with a very Young Church, there are hundreds of proven lay leaders. In each parish you have dozens. They already take over on the Sundays when the priest is absent. There is no reason to wait any longer."

"I also think we should press ahead as fast as possible, but my feeling is that we are still not ready for that enormous step."

"In what way are we not yet ready?"

"Let us take this particular country, this part of the Church. All priests and bishops have decided not even to introduce the permanent diaconate. They want lay leaders, but do not want to entrust them with anything permanent. More than that, they were sure there was no need even to discuss it with the communities. Not even the question of ordaining men, which is allowed, was discussed. Still less were we women ever considered. And you think they are ready to have lay leaders ordained priests? You are unrealistic."

"The diaconate was refused because it does not solve our real problem which is the frequent dearth of the Eucharist. Deacons can do next to nothing. Ordination to priesthood is a different matter. This is what we need. It will solve our problems and the Church should go ahead with it."

"Oh, I could not agree more with you, but you have to be realistic. You must see the problems we still have to overcome."

"You talk all the time of problems. There are no problems."

"No problems hah? Don't you know what is happening in the parishes? You have good lay leaders, yes, but in so many parishes you see one of them pushing himself forward. Do you think we would like to see these characters ordained? Neither the men nor we women want to be bossed around by such people. We must first learn how in our parishes we all can have a say in the selection of those who lead. Only then can we talk of ordinations."

"That will be solved very quickly. No need to wait any longer."

"Strange. Must it be me who has to tell you that there are plenty of other problems? What about your own confreres? Are they all convinced of their celibacy? H'm? What will they do if they hear that married lay leaders are to be ordained priests? Will they remain celibate? Do the bishops not have plenty of reason to fear that lots of them will try to get married then? You still see no problem?"

"It may affect one or the other priest..."

"Well, I think we better leave that topic. And in any case I am in a hurry to get to the post office."

It was the end of that dialog. Unfortunately many other dialogues on this topic end in the same fashion.

Some tried to force matters and had to give up

In the diocese of Y. there were many open-minded people and the bishop was surely one of them. Of the hundreds of parishes, almost all tried to work and pray together and to be a community Church. They were from old Catholic backgrounds and knew quite well what belonged to a life of faith.

The one thing that worried all Catholics was the declining number of priests. They were very distressed when, in one parish after the other, they were told that the bishop simply no longer had a priest for their parish, that on many Sundays the faithful themselves would have to conduct a Service of the Word instead of having Mass.

The matter was discussed at many meetings, sometimes among the lay leaders, sometimes with the priests and also the bishop. In this diocese the bishop and the priests were accustomed to discussing Church matters with the communities and their local leaders. They all agreed that in their diocese there was no problem about getting things done. There were dozens of lay workers in each parish, in bigger parishes more than a hundred. They were always willing to offer their services and they performed their tasks with joy. What they could not solve was the problem of people's frequent deprivation of the sacraments.

The Catholics were well informed in that part of the world and they were also aware of the discussions that were taking place at all levels of Church debate as to whether the shortage of priests could perhaps be solved by ordaining some married proven local leaders. There were plenty of proven lay leaders in their diocese but the bishop was not allowed to ordain them.

In meeting after meeting the faithful and the priests urged the bishop to go to Rome and plead for the permission for such ordinations. At the

World Synod of 1971 it had been made clear that in situations of pressing need the pope could give this permission. So, why not urge him to do so now?

The bishop initially disagreed. That request had already been turned down in several other dioceses. The shortages of priests in other parts of the world were more serious. If those dioceses did not succeed in getting that permission, there was no hope he would get it. One had to think of different ways.

Which different ways? Soon the idea gained ground that a kind of public pressure was necessary, not pressure in a bad sense but the creation of a kind of public urgency. The pope would have to be given compelling reasons, otherwise he could not agree. He could be accused by others of granting a far-reaching permission without necessity. It would have to be obvious that the pope reacted in order to solve a pressing need which everybody recognised as such.

First of all the case of their diocese would have to be a convincing one. Consequently the parishes began stepping up their formation. In each parish there had to be groups of very well-trained lay leaders. The bishop wrote pastoral letters about this training of lay leaders and emphasised that it was a response to the shortage of priests. The parishes cooperated well; the priests were unanimous in their support. Soon they would be ready to proceed to the step of publicity. How?

They finally agreed on the idea of the bishop writing an extraordinary pastoral letter. In his letter he would remind the whole diocese again of the shocking absence of the sacraments, would praise the parishes for their training of leaders who fulfilled most tasks formerly done by the priests and would then proceed to the crucial point. If the bishop saw that in certain parishes the need was really overwhelming, and if he were convinced that there was a proven married lay person who could be ordained, the bishop would personally present that person for ordination to the pope.

Not all agreed to this plan. A few priests, though in favour of the overall idea, were of the opinion that the strategy could not work. Pressure of this kind, even very gentle and humble pressure, could not succeed. The reason was not the stubbornness of the pope or his curia, but that they were dealing with a worldwide question. A permission of this kind would affect every corner of the Church. Most parts of the Church were by far not ready for such a step. In many parts of the world a permission of this kind would be misunderstood and misused. Even with the best will, the pope could not agree at this time and in the sole case of just their diocese. It was unfair to put pressure on him. The few priests who said so argued quite convincingly, but they did not prevail.

The pastoral letter was written. It attracted worldwide attention and achieved the publicity which was intended, but the matter ended there.

Twenty years later the idea is rejected.

Several countries of Africa were among those where the faithful suffered most severely because of the shortage of priests. Therefore, in 1970, twenty-five bishops of Cameroon, Gabon, Congo-Brazzaville, Chad, and the Central African Republic, wrote to Cardinal Villot, the then Secretary of State of the Vatican, and suggested: 1) to retain the law of priestly celibacy and not to allow marriage after ordination, but 2) to ordain *viri probati* in special circumstances. [1] The bishops did not receive a totally negative reply. They were told this could not be granted immediately, but it would be possible after some time if the pastoral situation necessitated it.

The bishops had good reason to ask for this permission to ordain proven local leaders. In their dioceses the new converts wanted to experience what a proper Christian life meant, and this included the regular Sunday Eucharist. It was clear to all that the initiation into a regular Eucharistic celebration was an essential part of evangelization. The shortage of priests in those years, the early seventies, was already so severe that the Eucharist was celebrated only once a month and even less frequently in some communities. The deliberations during the Second Vatican Council a few years earlier, 1962-1965, had indicated to those bishops that it was not totally impossible to ask for the introduction of the ordination of local *viri probati*, and so they made their request and received a fairly sympathetic reply.

Twenty years later the situation was different. Not the shortage of

---

[1]   Reported in DIE KATH.MISSIONEN 5/19/70, p. 149.

priests; that had meanwhile become even worse. What was different was the kind of bishops in charge of those dioceses. While in 1970 almost all had been expatriate members of missionary congregations, in the 1990's they were almost all indigenous bishops. In 1970 the vast majority of the priests had been expatriate missionaries with only very few indigenous priests; in the 1990's the great majority were indigenous priests.

Before the twenty-five bishops of 1970 presented their request to Rome, each one of them had many discussions with their priests and among themselves. The request to Rome was the result of these many consultations. The communities and their lay leaders were certainly not included in those discussions (in those days it had not yet dawned on Church leaders that this would be essential).

In the nineties there were and still are many consultations between bishops and priests. The shortage of priests and the ways of evangelization are discussed many times, but nobody or hardly anybody will suggest today to ordain *viri probati*. On the contrary, bishops and priests let it be known quite clearly that this idea is not welcome at all. Would it be welcome among lay leaders and their communities? We do not know because it is still not yet common to discuss such sensitive issues openly and among all. What we do know is that bishops and priests are now of a different opinion on this matter.

What a change in as little as twenty years! Further on we will reflect in more detail about the reasons why this idea of ordaining *viri probati* priests is not welcome in some young Churches in spite of the severe shortage of priests, and about the fact that in certain other types of young Churches the leaders are convinced of it. At this moment we just marvel at the rapid change of mind which did occur. Why do top level leaders see the same situation in such a different way?

Some thought it would be too expensive, while others knew it was the cheapest way

We are told that in another country the problem of the shortage of priests was also debated on the highest levels. Was it feasible to ask for permission to ordain proven local leaders to alleviate this shortage? It was well known that in all parishes there were many proven reliable leaders who might be suitable for such ordinations. They were married and followed a civil profession, and yet were spending much of their free time for their parish. These leaders fulfilled many tasks in the parish by voluntary work. They already conducted a service of the Word on those Sundays when the priest was unable to be present. They were already leading the local community in place of the priests most of the time. They were the actual leaders of the community. Why not seek permission to ordain them priests?

However, the bishops of that country saw one major obstacle which caused them to abandon the idea. They foresaw that they would be unable to finance it. In their reflections on the feasibility of that idea they had, of course, to rely completely on speculation, because nowhere in the Church of recent times had this proposal been put into practice. The bishops knew of the example of the early Church. That example was not helpful in their situation because times were now very different. Almost two thousand years had passed since, in the Early Church, practically all Church offices were executed by voluntary work. In those early days all bishops were part time workers, all priests and deacons lived by their own profession. The whole Church hierarchy consisted of *"viri probati"* and nobody thought of demanding a salary from the other members of the Church.

While in the early Church there was no question of remuneration for Church services, this was a fact now in our own time. People had become used to the model of the priest who was very different from the other members of the community. He had to be set apart. He therefore had to receive his formation far removed from others, had to dress differently, to live differently, and should surely not support himself by the work of his hands.

Of course, the shortage of priests had in recent years created a new kind of Church worker, the voluntary lay leader. There were several of them in each parish and none of them dreamt of asking for a penny for the hundreds of hours each one spent for the local community. Remuneration for lay leaders was never an issue because they were all aware that it was difficult enough to support the few existing priests financially. The priests had no family to support, were prepared to live on meagre allowances, and yet it was difficult to collect sufficient funds to support them. Nobody would even dream of creating additional expenses by paying lay workers with their families.

But what would happen if here and there one of those voluntary lay workers would be ordained priest? This was the crucial question. It was clear that those candidates would be asked whether they were willing to continue working as unpaid, voluntary workers as before, even after ordination. Initially they would most likely promise not to ask for remuneration, but could they continue to keep to it? Was it not quite likely that after some time the faithful would heap more and more tasks on them? That was indeed likely because even now many of the faithful still clamoured for the good old times when the priests were numerous and did everything for the faithful. A large portion of the faithful were now fulfilling tasks by voluntary work but were just waiting for the moment when they could revert to the old system of being cared for the priest.

If one of the many voluntary lay workers became ill and could no longer work, or for some other reason became unemployed and was in need, everybody knew that such a lay worker could not claim support from his fellow Catholics. Would this position not change with the introduction of ordained *"viri probati"*? If one of them was ordained on the understanding that he would always find his livelihood through his own civil profession but later became ill or unemployed, would not the hierarchy be obliged to take responsibility for him and his dependents? Once there were several such cases of *viri probati* priests living by the financial support of the Church, would this not become a pattern?

It was these fears which finally convinced the bishops of that country not to pursue the ordination of *viri probati* any further. They were convinced it was not feasible in their circumstances of financial constraints. *Viri probati* would simply be too expensive.

What a strange contrast to the conclusions reached by several other Christian Churches. Many non-Catholic Churches live in poor countries and find it very difficult to support their clergy financially. The Anglican Church is one of those who suffered under the fact that in many places they were unable to celebrate the Eucharist every Sunday because it was impossible to raise the finance necessary to support a priest and his family in each of the smaller congregations. They looked for a solution.

Over the last century the Anglican Church gradually moved away from the idea that each priest had to be set apart to such an extent that he could not live from the work of his hands. They had to abandon their long and cherished tradition, and gradually accepted the idea of having a second kind of priest. They are known by various names. In some places these priests were called "auxiliary priests" while others spoke of "self-supporting priests" or of "non-stipendiary priests" and again others of "community priests." What is most important about this new kind of priest is that his presence has made it financially feasible to have a priest in each small congregation which can now have the Eucharist every Sunday. It is much cheaper and thus possible. If today one visits Anglican dioceses who have "community priests" and asks about the pros and cons of having this new kind of priest, one will soon hear that the decisive factor is that this system is definitely less expensive. One will also hear that they, too, were aware of the possibility that some self-supporting priests might later claim Church support. They have, however, succeeded in making this problematic development quite unlikely.

What a contrast to the conclusions reached by some Catholic bishops as described above. They reached opposite conclusions at the same time. Their deliberations took place during the very same years. The two groups of bishops did not know of each other's reflections and so reached contrary conclusions. What does this say to us?

An avalanche would follow! It cannot be done

Anne and Elsie, the two secretaries of the bishop met for a short coffee break.

"Have the two visiting bishops left already?"

"Yes, they left an hour ago."

"Quite an extraordinary visit, isn't it? Endless hours of discussions, and nobody was allowed to know why they were meeting. We, too, were asked not to tell anybody. Have you finished typing their final notes?"

"I have. And now I understand the reason for all that secrecy. Had the press known that they were talking for three days on that sensitive subject of *viri probati* the house would have been beleaguered by a crowd of journalists."

"I also understand now why our bishop invited only his two best friends for that topic. With any of the others he could not have talked freely about this topic."

"Yes, I understand. But tell me, what is your personal opinion about their conclusion? They say they will not pursue the matter any further for the foreseeable future. In their view it is not feasible at this time because it could start an avalanche of consequences, creating more damage than good. Do you agree with that?"

"I'm glad I am not a bishop. I don't know what I would have said."

"But you have studied theology for years. You are actively involved in your parish. You told me that you yourself had endless discussions on this same question with the other lay leaders of your parish. Even in the Diocesan Pastoral Council you yourself proposed that this step of ordaining *viri probati* should be taken. So what do you say now about the conclusion of our three bishops?"

"I can see their point to a certain extent. They say an avalanche of consequences would follow. I can understand that view. They see two dangers especially. One is the question of women. The bishops realize that the moment they would publicly favour the ordination of proven men there will the thousands of women who will say: You bishops have promised so loudly that you will overcome unequal treatment of women and now you do the opposite. You exclude the women from among the proven leaders. Don't you know that there are more proven women than proven men? There will even be parishes where the men will side with them and will say they are not prepared to be selected alone. Unless the women are also considered as candidates they will not cooperate."

"Yes, that is exactly what would happen; there would be protest throughout the whole country. There would be an outcry. It would lead to bitter confrontations because the bishops are bound by the prohibition from Rome and cannot give in. It would lead to a long fruitless confrontation. It would lead to more harm than good. You said there was a second danger?"

"The second one is equally tricky. It's the question what would happen to the many hundreds of 'pastoral assistants.' Unlike the women dilemma, that is a problem specific to central Europe, not to the whole world. But here it is crucial. Our Church in these countries always had a better financial position, at least until now. Therefore here we could afford to compensate for the shortage of priests through the employment of hundreds or thousands of pastoral assistants."

"My own brother is one of them."

"What does he feel about the ordination of *viri probati*? Does he see any problem?"

"For himself not. He would be quite willing to be ordained priest. His wife agrees and his parish would love to have him as their priest. They would much prefer to have him as their priest instead of waiting all the time for a neighbouring priest to come and administer the sacraments. He does not see a problem."

"I know. Most of them don't see a problem. It's the bishops who see a problem, and to some extent I can understand. Imagine the case of your own brother. If he were ordained priest the parish would rejoice. Then you have in the same town two pastors with their families, the Lutheran pastor and the Catholic priest, exactly the same."

"And what's the problem with that?"

"The problem is that if that happens then we have not moved one inch ahead. We will have copied the Lutheran parish, nothing more. We have not moved away an inch from our passive parish life. Until now it was a celibate priest who cared for the passive crowd, and from then on it will be a married one. No step forward. We would have missed our chance to move a great step ahead, to stop being provided by a pastor from above, start doing things ourselves, celebrating the sacraments with some from among ourselves, the liturgy and the whole community being led by some of us who live like we live. That would be a step forward. That's what I want, and what many others want."

"Is that what the bishops want? Is that why they refused to go ahead with *viri probati*?"

"I think so. They at least realize that if at this moment the ordination of *viri probati* is raised here in central Europe, there will be no search for community candidates. It is because there are already obvious candidates. They are so obvious that the parishes will refuse to look for anybody else; the press will say the same. No reflection on other structures would happen. We would be caught in a trap."

"I often hear my brother saying he would not be caught in this trap. He would lead the parish to become active, to bring forth many leaders, to share all tasks with them. He would not become a monopolising priest."

"I know him. He is quite an exception. Many others would not act like him, and I think our bishops know this. That is why they say this is not the time to move ahead."

"My brother told me a few times that they have meetings among the pastoral assistants and several of them are becoming aware that their role is crucial at this time. They can make or break the movement towards the development of a community Church."

"Thanks be to God that this movement has started a bit. It is also helped by the recent signs of a financial shortage in all dioceses. Everybody is slowly beginning to realize that the solution must lie somewhere besides the employment of more personnel, not in getting more full-time priests alone but in increasing the voluntary leaders. But at this moment we have only just started with this development. It is far too early to rely on it. It needs to be consolidated."

"You mean to say our three bishops were right in their postponement?"

"Somehow I think they were. These three bishops are well known as the three most progressive ones in the country. They have probably tried to look with some optimism at this question of *viri probati*, but in whatever way they looked at it, they always came back to the conclusion that it is not feasible at this moment. I hope it will change soon."

"Oh, it's high time to continue typing. I'll talk to you later."

* * *

Many have argued for and against. Let's consider this important question in more detail.

Part Two

The Choices Before Us

Different versions or different visions?

Most suggestions to ordain viri probati date back to the time of the Second Vatican Council. During the Council some bishops proposed such ordinations, but it was decided to remove the topic from the agenda of the Council and to deal with it at a later stage. This was then done during the World Synod of Bishops in 1971 when about 45% of the delegated bishops voted in favour of ordaining *viri probati.*

What type of viri probati did the bishops foresee at that time? They didn't specify, but we can assume that they had in mind what was most commonly described in the contemporary publications. The suggestions made then are almost exclusively contained in Options 1 and 2 reviewed below. But at that time no attempt was made to distinguish between different options or different visions of *viri probati.* Those who suggested *viri probati* probably thought everybody meant the same thing when proposing such ordinations. It is only in retrospect that we can assign their ideas to different categories or options.

Even today those reflecting on the possibility of ordaining *viri probati* are giving the impression that they mean one and the same thing, but is this true? Are we merely differing in minor details or, in fact, pursuing very different goals? Are we considering slightly differing versions of the same movement, all of which lead us in the same direction, or are we faced with choices which involve divergent paths and consequently opposing views? Are we dealing with fundamentally different visions?

Is there not the danger that, without realizing it, we lend our support to an idea which we will one day reject? Where people use the term *"viri probati"* with different meanings, behind the different usage of the same term there may be a different target vision.

Therefore, in this second part, we will first try to describe the different ways in which *"viri probati"* have been suggested, then consider the serious implications of choosing among them, then make our own choice. In Part Three we will endeavour to show how our preferred model could realistically be put into practice.

The publications dealing with the introduction of *viri probati* contain varying suggestions that could be grouped into many categories, but there seem to be three distinct trends. The first trend is to ordain some of those who are already in some way employed by the Church; the second is to ordain one of the voluntary leaders in each of the communities; and the third trend is to ordain a team of voluntary leaders in each community.

Each of these three trends has been proposed in several different nuances, so we therefore have to speak of three main options and several sub-options. Each of the options has to be described in some detail including its pros and cons. Before doing this an overview of these three options and their nuances is given.

Different types of viri probati priests: the main options and sub-options.

Option 1: Ordaining employed Church workers:

1a. Pastoral Assistants: They have received full theological training, are employed full-time by the Church and can be transferred.

1b. Trained Pastor-Catechists: They have received partial training, are employed full-time by the Church and can be transferred.

1c. Trained Pastor-Catechists who have received partial training, are fully or partly employed by the Church but cannot be transferred (because they partly live from another profession or live on their own land or for similar reasons).

This first group of suggestions has in common that the ordained person is financially dependent on the Church and the bonds of belonging are therefore stronger towards the hierarchy than towards the people.

Option 2: Ordaining one voluntary leader in many communities:

2a. One leader is ordained from teams which emerged from an active community and fulfill almost all the services in the community. The leaders have intensive bonds towards the community, but less so towards the priest who has to serve many distant communities.

2b. One member of a "Pastoral Team" which includes the priest and is serving several passive congregations is ordained. The team members are united by intensive bonds towards one another, but less so towards the congregation. The priest is frequently present in the team.

2c. One leader who serves a passive congregation and does not have close bonds towards the congregation or the priest or a pastoral team is ordained. It was often suggested this could be a good Catholic who is a retired person. Bonds of belonging are not structured and depend purely on each one's personality and conviction.

Common to this second group of suggestions is the ordained person's financial independence. The bonds of belonging differ vastly.

Option 3: Ordaining teams of community leaders:

Not *one* person is ordained in a community but a *team* of community leaders who have proven over a long time that they can cooperate well with the active community from whom they have emerged and with the priests who accompany them.

There are no real sub-options in this case because such teams can emerge only from an active community, must be self-supporting and non-transferable. Differences lie only in minor aspects.

The above overview shows that the idea of a "leader" can be understood in different ways, that a "team" can mean different things (2b versus 3), and that there are significant differences among the varying bonds of belonging.

It is our opinion that these three main visions underlie the many different suggestions. Now we will give a more detailed description of the main options and also the difficulties, questions, hopes and fears associated with each of them. We will show why the choice among these options is probably a "no-return" decision and why we do not consider the three options as successive stages towards a final solution. Therefore we have grouped the suggestions into three options and rather than to compile one long list of the various suggestions. We have been guided by the conviction that the choice among the three main options has very serious consequences. It is for this reason that we emphasize the need for many study groups to consider the different options and their implications.

Option 1:
Ordaining employed Church workers.

Many would never dream of considering this option as the first one, but for others it was in fact the first and only possibility they could think of. We will begin by trying to understand, then consider its value.

The shortage of priests has prompted the Church in several parts of the world to employ lay persons as pastoral workers and often even as leaders of the local Christian community which has no priest. This was and is done in different forms in different countries. In financially strong countries the Church employed highly trained and professionally paid "pastoral assistants," while in less developed countries the Church employed partly trained, poorly paid "catechists" whom one should rather call "pastor-catechists" because their role is usually more pastoral than catechetical. Not all of the Young Churches have followed this method nor did all of the Old Churches do so. Choices depended on the overall outlook of the Church in that area and also on its financial means.

Whatever the difference in training and in payment, the common factor is that those persons employed are more dependent on the priest than on the community, and that they often do for the community what the community could actually do by itself but does not want to do.

Where such employed lay pastors serve a community which has no priest, they conduct the Service of the Word on Sundays, conduct the funerals, visit the sick, conduct catechesis and do whatever can be done without ordination. In the Older Church one parish or one cluster parish may have one or two employed lay pastors of this kind, while in the young Churches it may have up to ten or even more.

The pastoral result of this method of employing lay pastors is that some of the immediate pastoral needs are fulfilled, that the sacraments remain nevertheless rare, that the faithful remain in their traditional attitude of being provided for, that the priests tend to develop more an attitude of administration and control and less of community building. This was and is the situation of some areas where the idea of possibly ordaining an additional kind of priest began to surface.

When in 1970 twenty five bishops of Central Africa asked for permission to ordain *viri probati*, they were probably thinking of ordaining village catechists. We find the same suggestion in many publications . It could be significant that the cover picture of one of these publications shows an auxiliary priest of this envisaged type in black cassock and stole, as a real cleric, with a golden wedding ring above his head.[2]

What hopes have been pinned on Option 1? What problems are associated with it? What questions arise? The main question is: to what kind of Church will this type of *viri probati* lead us?

This Option surely alleviates the scarcity of the sacraments, but it perpetuates the vision of a clergy-led Church. The Protestant Churches had a like clergy of married, Church-employed ministers for a long time and remain a clergy-led Church although they originally intended to abolish precisely

---

[2] Raymond Hickey, "Africa, the case for an auxiliary priesthood", Geoffrey Chapman/ London 1980. Hickey is aware of the diverse usage of the term "catechist" in Africa and does not suggest the ordination of all catechists but of one trained catechist for each sub-parish, as its auxiliary priest (p.79). Hickey's whole book is devoted to the ordination of catechists. Other authors are less elaborate but suggest the same pattern. In Kinshasa, Zaire, the difference is that they envisage one voluntary leader, called "mokambi", to be ordained.

this type of clergy. It is interesting to note that several Protestant Churches had at one time or another reflected on the possibility of introducing "tent-maker" ministry in order to overcome the paradigm of a clericalised Church. In some countries of the First World where the Catholic Church is at this moment considering *viri probati* priests, the Protestant Church has no intention at all to do so. The reason for the contrast is that the Catholic parishes are suffering from a severe shortage of priests while at the same time the Protestant Church has a pastor in even the smallest village. The high number of employed pastors is thus an obstacle against moving towards the desired ideal of a community-Church. If the Catholic Church ordains Church-employed personnel, will it not move in the same wrong direction?

In the case of the Young Churches, there is the further danger of introducing employed priests of lower education, a situation which proved problematic in the middle ages. Priests of that kind would be averse to social change, would disapprove of modern theology and resent any increased role of the educated laity and would prefer an inflexible, "other-worldly" liturgy.

A further drawback of this option, especially in areas of the Younger Churches, is that it perpetuates attitudes of employment. The pastor-catechist of those areas has often been described, even by papal encyclicals, as the "prolonged arm of the priest." There have been some saintly catechists and saintly priests in those areas, but there has also been a much greater number who suffered under this employment relationship. In areas where there is a huge gap of education and material means and where employment was not legally regulated and could easily be exploited, there has been much suffering, bitterness and discontent on both sides. If there is any chance to make a new start and to build up different relationships, it should be done. There is certainly no reason to prolong the harmful patterns and to solidify them through the widespread ordination of employed lay pastors.

To implement this option would, in many countries, also mean a great increase in financial expenditure. Only in some parts of Central Europe where the "pastoral assistants" already receive full family remuneration would there be no increased financial burden. In other countries, both in the older and in the Younger Churches, this option would be almost impossible from the financial point of view.

One advantage in ordaining fully employed Church workers is that they can be transferred. The need for a transfer could arise when the time comes to introduce a different type of *viri probati*, or when a particular person is needed elsewhere or has become unsuitable in his present position. It is only the partly-employed persons who cannot be transferred (Option 1c) because they live partly from their own means of income which ties them to the place of their livelihood.

Option 2:
Ordaining one voluntary leader in many communities

This option arose where the communities did not rely on remunerated, employed lay pastors but rather on voluntary leaders. Long before anybody thought of ordaining local leaders the communities and their priests wanted to live their Christian life by sharing tasks and decisions. People were invited to work for the community through voluntary work, not through employment. The priests animated and trained the emerging leaders and this led to each community having a number of leaders. The sacraments did, however, remain rare because the priest had to serve several such active communities and their leaders. In Young Churches, one priest may serve ten chapel-communities, or three priests serve up to thirty and forty. In older Churches with a shortage of priests, one priests may serve three, four or more chapel-communities/parishes.

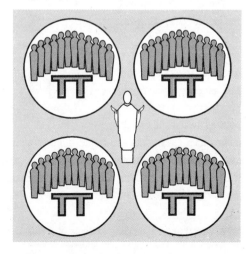

When the possibility of ordaining local leaders appeared, several different suggestions were made. The nuances between those suggestions may sound confusing, so we have tried to depict those differing proposals in the form of diagrams. In order to make the comparison easier, we show each priest as serving four communities. These communities may symbolize a situation where four neighbouring former parishes and their leaders were now served by one priest. The symbol could also stand for a parish of a large area in one of the Young Churches, where one or two priests had to serve ten or twenty "outstations", each having its small church and its leaders.

The above diagram, which depicts the situation of the communities relevant to option 2a, shows the peculiar fact that there are many active lay persons *next* to the altar, but the place at the altar remains empty. This situation differs from the one of Option 1 in two important features. There is no "prolonged arm of the priest" in each congregation and the active laity are themselves already conducting the para-liturgies for which they have received training. That is, the idea of sharing ministries already exists – the community itself is responsible for its life and its liturgy. Many of the bishops who have jurisdiction over this genre of Church see the need of filling the empty place at the altar.

Let us now turn to the variety of ways in which the ordination of *viri probati* priests was suggested, all of them falling within this option 2. The first thing we will notice is that they all seem to agree on one point. In the multitude of short articles, speeches and meetings where the shortage of priests was pointed out while, at the 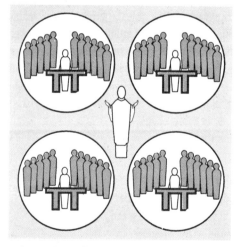 same time, there was an ample number of many active lay ministers, a consensus of opinion was expressed in the resolve: "We will find among those many leaders one who can be entrusted with presiding over the Eucharist."[3] It seems strange that they reached the same decision: to find

---

[3]   A typical and outstanding example of a diocese which has this kind of ordina-

one person, but it is a fact that they all did so. They were probably guided by the all too familiar sight of always having one priest at the altar.

Had they grown up in the communities of New Testament times, they would not have envisioned *one* person presiding alone. In our lifetime, this is the only picture we have known and therefore even the Young Churches, although they are accustomed to sharing many charisms in the community, envisage the ordaining of *one* person.

Where it is Older Churches which feel inclined towards Option 2, the diagram must often take a different form. There is no group of active leaders next to that empty altar. Tasks are fulfilled not by those local leaders but in a different way. A central "mixed team" is formed consisting of the priest and several active lay

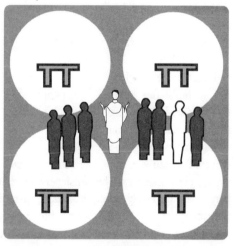

people, all of whom are voluntary workers. The team meets often, plans together, prays together and serves the needs of the rather passive congregations. It has been suggested that *one* member of the mixed team be ordained priest to minister not just to one congregation but to all those served by the team. This will increase the number of priests in the mixed team from one to two. The bonds of belonging experienced by that *vir probatus* priest will be stronger towards the mixed inter-parish team than to one particular congregation. This is why the diagram placed him within the mixed team, not within one of the parishes. He may preside over the sacraments in any of the congregations, perhaps on an alternating basis. (This kind of mixed team is very different from the teams on which option 3 is based.) — There are of course areas where there is not a complete

---

tion in mind is the report given by Bishop G. Cloin of Barra, Bahia, Brazil, "A new kind of priest" in PMV Bulletin No. 50, 1974, p. 73-76.

vacuum around the empty altar but there are at least a few active people at each place.

There is a third version of option 2 (Option 2c, p. 59), also voiced in dioceses of the Older Churches. The scarcity of the sacraments could be ameliorated by ordaining an outstanding Catholic who has the proven faith and the theological education to fulfill this ministry. In our diagram that person is shown serving mainly one congregation.

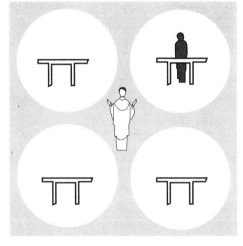

It would be fairly easy to find such a person among the professionals or among the pensioners. The pensioners are mentioned quite often because they would obviously be more available than others. We do of course note that this priest could probably not rely on any structured relationship. It may depend totally on good luck that a relationship to the community and to the priest is established.

What are the questions likely to arise from option 2? To what kind of Church will it lead us? ·

As in option 1, option 2 will alleviate the scarcity of the Sacraments. Those who promote it are aware that not every congregation will find a suitable candidate. As with the other options, there will be congregations which for many years will still depend for the sacraments on the animator priest while others already have their ordained local leader.

Option 2 will not cause the financial difficulties inherent in option 1 and it does not envisage a clerical type of priest, at least not in its original intention. It can, however, lead to a similar difficulty – the difficulty that an ordained *vir probatus* later becomes unbearable and there is no way of removing him because he permanently resides in the parish area. He may develop clericalistic attitudes or in other ways prove unsuitable.

This problem is realized by the very ones who made the suggestion, especially those who favour Option 2a. They have gone through many years of community building and are well aware that almost any leader can become unsuitable. They speak mainly of the danger of a leader becoming a domineering person, no longer acceptable to the community. There are, of course, other reasons why an ordained leader might become unsuited to the community. He could later prove out of step with the changing times, or develop an improper life-style, or get into leadership conflicts which could not be resolved.

Those who propose the ordination of this type of *viri probati* are aware that the problem of a *vir probatus* priest becoming unsuitable cannot be solved in the traditional way of transferring him to another parish. He does not depend on the Church financially but on his secular occupation, so cannot be transferred.

The promoters of this option have, therefore, had to resort to strange solutions. They suggest avoiding ordination altogether and, instead, granting a temporary permission to the *viri probati* to preside over the Eucharist. This would make it possible for them to be replaced.[4] While probably very few will take this suggested solution seriously, the problem they point out is real and shows the weakness of ordaining only one lay person in a community.

Where only one voluntary person is ordained, there is the possibility and even probability of his becoming overburdened. Instead of asking for the ordination of a second and even third person to share his priestly duties, he might decide to relinquish his secular work and insist on being remunerated by the Church. This would not only cause a financial burden but would make this second option identical with the first one with its inherent problems.

The same problem can arise in a different way. In some smaller Protestant Churches experience showed that congregations which were served by one part-time minister tried after some time to make him a full-time one. The reason was not that the congregation was too large to be served adequately by a part-time minister but it was the desire of the congregation to become a respectable Church which has a "normal" minister. People

---

4   Pro Mundi Vita Bulletin No. 50 of 1974, p. 63 and 65.

were asked to make additional financial contributions in spite of their poverty in order to make the part-time minister a full-time one. They spent
money without need, only in order to acquire a higher status. It shows us
that it is not so easy to uphold the ideal of voluntary, community-based
ministry. If we introduce a new kind of ordination we will do well to move
away from status ideas and to ensure we emphasise community building.

A further danger is that communities which opt for the ordination of
one person may favour an older person. They have good reason to do so
because he will be the only priest in this congregation for the time of his
life. Will the choice of older men in all parishes not lead to an unacceptable image of a Church, one that belongs to the older generation, a kind of
"pensioner-Church"? Can it not make the Church outdated if that older
person continues for many years and is not easy to replace? Replacing an
older person is quite difficult because many members of the community
will hesitate to offend that person and his relatives.

Option 2 may be workable in a few lucky cases but as a general
solution it is fraught with too many problems.

Option 3:
Ordaining teams of community leaders

Only very few people have up to now proposed moving in a different
direction and opting for the ordination of teams of viri probati for each
community.[5]

The suggestions never to ordain *one* leader alone but only teams of
viri probati have, understandably, been made only in areas where congregations have experienced progressive stages of community building. A diagram depicting option 3 will, therefore, show not only teams of ordained
leaders at the altar but also teams of other community leaders next to
them.

---

[5]   The Southern African Catholic Bishops Conference commissioned a study on the
      crisis in ministry and stated its preference for the ordination of teams rather
      than individuals. "The Transformation of the Ministry" 1971, SACBC General
      Secretariat, P.O. Box 941, Pretoria 0001.

Those who promote this Option are convinced that the presence of many other active teams, as well as the one at the altar, is an essential element of the congregation. They consider it vital that the few ordained ones come from the ranks of the many who have been community leaders for many years. All of them wanted to assist the com- 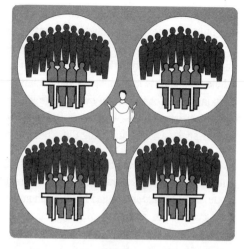 munity; they did not aim at priesthood. They do not have a clericalistic outlook; they have proved over many years that their style of leadership is a non-dominating one seeking the cooperation of the whole community. In a healthy community the domineering characters are less likely to be successful, although one can expect to find some exceptions. Furthermore, having a team of ordained leaders offers the constant possibility of new candidates emerging from the community to join the team. There is a greater chance than in option 2 that the changing times and the concerns of society will be reflected in the team of ordained leaders.

It is not unrealistic to consider ordaining teams. In dioceses of young Churches the existence of several teams of active leaders in each parish is the norm, while in Old Churches it is the exception.

Bishop J. Van Cauwelaert, in his lecture to the 44th Missiology Week of Louvain 1974. Title "Les catechistes, collaborateurs efficaces de l'ordre sacerdotal", No. 6, p. 28.

From Lutheran Missions in Malaysia it is reported that unremunerated local leaders were ordained in an emergency situation, but in such a way that only teams of three could administer the sacraments together. (Evangelisches Missions Magazin 1/1971 23-30, esp. 26-27). A later unpublished report I received in 1993 on 40 years of this experience speaks of 110 such ordinations having taken place.

It is also suggested in one of the latest publications on this topic by P. Zulehner, "Europe without Priests?" ed. by J. Kerkhofs, SCM 1995, 178.

The above diagram shows the teams of four viri probati priests and also the full-time priest who brought them into existence. He lived in one of the parishes, serving several others and their teams of leaders during the years that led up to the ordination of the first *viri probati*. His role in leading the whole area and its many helpers and leaders to this point was essential and remains so; he continues to oversee the whole process, to form lay leaders and the ordained ones. Whereas in Old Churches a priest may care for three or four such parishes, in Young Churches he serves ten and even more.

In the diagrammatic presentation of the initial stage of option 3, the one priest serving several scattered congregations continues to function alone as an animator. He has led the communities towards the stage where they could form teams of ordained community leaders. The diagram is symbolic and shows four communities with four ordained leaders each. The reality will be different in each place. The one priest might serve ten communities but only eight of them have succeeded – some having a team of four ordained leaders, others three or only two, while some may remain having no ordained leaders as yet. In those communities the animator priest is still the only one who administers the sacraments; he continues to lead them to the stage when their own teams will be ordained.

It is most likely that such a full-time priest will not continue to live alone among the many communities he serves. He will eventually prefer to live and work as a team with other animators. Our diagram shows a team of three animator priests amidst four pastoral areas formerly called "parishes." The animator priests assist a large number of communities, most of which have a considerable number of ordained lay leaders.

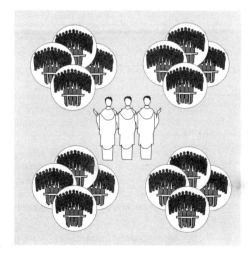

In the diagram we see two kinds of priest –

the many small teams of ordained leaders and the one team of three animator priests who serve the four former parishes with their communities, a total of twenty, forty or more communities. We will later discuss the question of finding a suitable name which distinguishes the accustomed full-time priest from the new type of ordained local leaders. Both are priests but their work is different. Since the full-time priests work mainly as animators we may perhaps call them "animator priests".

In addition to the team of animator priests there may be other groups (not shown in the diagram) who fulfill an animating and assisting role for the surrounding communities. In many places such groups already exist. Often the team consists of religious but it could also be a group of lay people.

The task of the animation teams will mainly be the ongoing formation of the *viri probati* priests, the formation of new candidates, the formation and training of the many teams of other leaders, the settling of disputes in the name of the bishop, and other kinds of assistance which the communities need. The teams exercise part of the task of the bishop as the "overseer" of the life of the local Church. In his name they animate the many communities.

The earlier diagrams of Option 3 showed, in a symbolic way, four communities per animator priest. In reality an animator or a team of animators will often serve a large number of communities. Once the ordination of leaders has spread, a team of animators may, especially in Young Churches, serve a great number of communities spread over a wide area. We can assume that a team may serve thirty or fifty communities, each having two, three or more ordained leaders, plus

some communities which did not yet reach the stage of having ordained leaders. A team of animators may therefore accompany even a hundred ordained leaders.

In spite of such high numeric relationships it is realistic to assign such a role to teams of animator priests. It is something that exists already in many Young Churches and that will not become fundamentally different after the ordination of teams of *viri probati* priests. In many parishes of developing countries today, a team of three priests is serving forty and fifty "outstations" by administering all sacraments plus all organizational work and the work of training the lay leaders. In a way, the task of overseeing the communities will become easier after the ordination of leaders because the animator priests will no longer be overburdened with the celebration of all Sacraments in so many communities. In another way it will be more demanding, since they will be dealing with ordained teams who have received a definite authority. We will deal with this aspect in more detail later.

The work of *viri probati* teams comprises much more than the celebration of the sacraments. Ordination to the priesthood means accepting the responsibility of leading the community in its will to follow the Gospel. The teams direct the life of the community, constitute its unifying principle, and maintain the link of the local community to the universal Church. Just as the present priest is usually not the chairperson of his parish council but, nevertheless, presides over it, the teams of *viri probati* priests will fulfill the same function.

A review of the existing patterns in the Young Churches gives credence to the possibility of team leadership. It does not presume to be something completely new but merely the completion of an existing reality.

The formation and selection of candidates for *viri probati* will take place not in a remote training institution but mainly in their home community. They have a family and an occupation, hence their formation will be limited to evenings and some weekends. From time to time there may also be short training courses of a whole week, but no long residential formation in a training institute, which is not only impossible but also undesirable because it would alienate the candidates from their community.

Community-based formation of this kind is already happening in the Young Churches and has proved successful. Those who begin such a process are not entering it for the sake of becoming ordained but with the sole purpose of doing something for the community. They go through ten or more years of service to the community, fulfilling a variety of tasks and learning what they can use immediately. They do not follow a clearly mapped out syllabus during the first years. Only during the final years of formation will the question of ordination be considered and the training will then become more systematic.

The formation of permanent deacons generated a wealth of experience in this field. It became clear that it is important to begin training without aiming at a specific office or specifying a length of time for formation. Such methodology could lead to a "ladder of promotion," a "right" to be ordained after a certain time or after passing prescribed academic examinations and, on the other hand, to negative feelings on the part of those who find it better to withdraw during the process.

The selection of candidates is similar. It is community based. The candidates emerge gradually from among the active people of the community. Many people are engaged in the early stages of selection, and even the final process requires the cooperation of the formation personnel, the parish council, the wives of the candidates, and the bishop. Selection is certainly not based on academic examinations but on the presence of a charism and the ability to serve and lead this particular community.

What positives does this option offer? What problems should we foresee?

Option 3 presents an image of Church where the ordained ministry is not a separate class but is woven into the believing community, a situation highly desirable to some but deeply threatening to others. It is an option in the true sense, not just a stop-gap solution as in the case of the first two options. This is its strength, but it entails a leap forward which many may judge to be too radical. Those who wish to move forward towards a Church where the ordained are "like the brothers and sisters" (Hebr 2, 17) will certainly prefer this option.

Some of the problems inherent in the first two options are solved in the third one. A clerical type of *viri probati* priests is unlikely, and the withdrawal of ordained community leaders who have become unacceptable is much easier. A structure of this kind easily adjusts to changing times. The teams of priests are open to new members so that the Church is less likely to become outdated.

The challenge of maintaining a high standard among the *viri probati* priests and of keeping them united with the bishop will remain major tasks, though less difficult in the third option than in the other two options. New procedures will be necessary. In a later chapter we offer some suggestions in this regard.

As we considered the various ways in which the ordination of *viri probati* priests has been suggested and as we tried to understand these different options, we encountered several difficulties. We will now try to deal with some of them. We will speak about the difficulty of finding the most suitable terminology. We surely find the term "*viri probati* priests" not easy and we will try to find a better term. We will then consider the usefulness – or the of lack of it – of another problematic term which has often been used in connection with the ordination of married proven Christians, the term "optional celibacy". Following this we will respond to those who may feel these proposals might be similar to failed attempts made in history and in different parts of the Church. With these short sections we wish to further clarify the specific proposals to ordain local proven leaders.

New kinds of priest need new terminology

During the above descriptions of the various options we made use of different terminology, sometimes referring to "*viri probati* priests" and at other times to "ordained leaders." We are not alone in this difficulty. The various authors and groups who dealt with the subject have all tried in different ways to use new terminology.

There have always been different kinds of priest in the Catholic Church and yet there has been no need to use different names to distinguish them. There are the highly learned theologians and at the same time the simple village priests. Many priests serve alone in a parish for their whole life; others fulfill specialized tasks in a seminary or university. In spite of this diversity the question of differentiating by way of different names, of inventing a new terminology for a new role has not arisen before.

It does, however, seem that there will be a need for new terminology once we introduce ordained community leaders. The reason is that there will then be two kinds of priest who continuously work in an interdependent way. We therefore have to distinguish continuously between the priests ordained to serve only their home community and the others who are their diocesan animators.

When the first moves were made in introducing new types of priests, mainly in other Churches, various classifications were suggested. Some wanted to call the new type "tent-maker priests", highlighting the way St. Paul supported himself and seeing this as the point of change. Others spoke of "supplementary priests," "auxiliary priests," "non-stipendiary priests." Further suggestions were "self-supporting priests" as distinct from "Church-supported priests," and "part-time priests" as against "full-time priests." In the Catholic Church we have not yet moved beyond the Latin *"viri probati."* In some Anglican dioceses and in a few Catholic publications the term "community priests" has been used.

The search for a suitable term is still on. We might end up choosing a biblical term such as "Corinth-priest" or "Corinth-leader" in order to distinguish the type of community-related vocation (emerging out of active community life) from the type of call which Paul received (not originating from a community but sent to many communities).

We have already pointed out the need in many groups to discuss the future continuous interaction between these two types of priest. For these many discussion meetings we should find a complementary and easy pair of terms to name the two types. The terms need to be short and at the same time significant in order to become widely used. One possibility is a biblical pair of terms such as "Corinth-priests" and "Paul-priests." They would express the complementarity of roles. The Corinth-priests are stationary. They emerge from one community and serve mainly this one community. The Paul-priests move. They serve many communities, animating and uniting them. An additional advantage of a pair of biblical terms is the fact that the terms will remain untranslated when a multiplicity of languages are used.

It is difficult to find the right word for the existing kind of priests who work full-time and can be transferred. To call them by the term "full-time priests" sometimes arouses opposition because all priests possess their priesthood at all times, whether they are engaged in secular work or in liturgical service. The term "animator priests" which signifies their new role might have a good chance of being widely accepted. The most meaningful classification for full-time priests would, of course, be the well-known "diocesan priests" as they work for the whole diocese, are at the very centre of the diocesan structure and may be moved from parish to parish within the diocese, while the "community priests" or "community leaders" are stationary, serving only their own community. The term "diocesan priests" has, however, always been used to distinguish secular priests from priests of religious institutes, so a change in the accepted meaning of the phrase would be quite confusing. It could certainly not be used in the beginning phase of two kinds of priest though it might well become suitable later.

The importance of the terminology is affected by the choice made among the main options outlined above. Where option 1 or 2 is favoured, a distinguishing name for the new kind of priest is not a major concern. Where the preference is option 3, it is crucial. This choice aims at a new image of Church and the terminology should indicate this. "Ordained community leaders" is not only an apt description but would probably also be very acceptable to the candidates themselves and this is an important consideration.

It will be important to choose a term which fits easily into the daily lives of the community leaders. Their daily life is spent in the family circle, with friends, and at the work place; for them it is more important to be known by a terminology which is socially acceptable rather than by one which is theologically precise. The term "ordained community leaders" avoids the cultic word "priest" but nevertheless contains the meaning; those three simple words are saying rather well what was meant by the word "presbyter" in the early Church. The term consists of three words and is too long for daily conversations. If the term is chosen then it will automatically be shortened to "community leader" in daily life while theological literature will use the full term "ordained community leader."

The term chosen should be suitable for people who live like anybody else. It should avoid reference to an otherworldly, different class. It should be suitable for ordained leaders who never wear clerical dress. It is our desire that the new kind of priest should not just supplement and imitate the existing priests but should be different from them and should be "like the brothers and sisters" (Hebr 2, 17).

It is obvious that all the above suggestions have drawbacks. It is impossible to find exact distinguishing terms pertinent to every place and situation. There will always be exceptional cases for which a particular distinction will not fit.

Mindful of all this, when describing the processes of introducing Option 3, we will in Part Three make extensive use of the term "ordained community leader" (OCL) although we have not yet made our final choice among the many terms. The term expresses well what we intend but is rather lengthy. An acronym such as OCL may be acceptable in a publication but it will not become popular in community discussions. We rather have to wait to see which term will finally win.

The phrase "optional celibacy" is misleading

There is another term which might confuse the discussion. It is the term "optional celibacy". Many have tried to describe the future diversification of priesthood by this term, but after our initial explanation of the most likely models of ordained community leaders it becomes clear that this phrase is more misleading than helpful. It is misleading in several ways.

The phrase is misleading because it leads people to think that the main question is whether priests should be celibate or not. In our time the main question is a different one: how we can be Church together.

"Optional celibacy" is misleading because it gives the impression that the model of the provider-priest caring for a passive congregation will continue. All that will change is his celibate state; every candidate for priesthood will – as the term suggests – have the choice of becoming either a celibate or a married priest. In reality it is just the other way round. What is being abandoned is the idea of the provider-priest while the principle of total self-giving will remain a high ideal in the Church.

It is understandable that the phrase was coined to indicate a new era where there will be different kinds of priest, in contrast to the time when there was only one kind and when the only access to priesthood was via the vow of celibacy. Thus it is true there will now be a plurality of priesthood options that did not exist before. However, the term "optional celibacy" fails to describe this new situation adequately.

If one day the parishes will have OCLs in the way explained above, one cannot really say that each of these ordained married leaders made an "option" to become a married priest. At the time when they got married they made no option and did not even think of becoming a priest. That idea came to them much later, after many years of active involvement in the Christian community. When they decided to offer themselves as *viri probati* priests, they made no option between celibate or married priesthood because they were already married.

For the Christian community of the future one can also not say that they are "opting" for married, part-time priests. Whether candidates for OCLs are married or celibate will not be their point of interest. They will rather be interested in a very different question: "How do we find among ourselves those able and willing to accept full responsibility for the Gospel? Who can give us an example of living the gospel? Who can best help us live the Gospel in our community?" That is their chief interest. Communities will even be very reluctant to accept unmarried community leaders and the idea of such an option is far from their minds. The term "optional celibacy" has no meaning in their context.

On the diocesan level, "optional celibacy" is again unhelpful and misleading because it does not express the real concern of the dioceses. In future the dioceses' priority will be: "Can this animator priest inspire, accompany, train and assist the ordained local leaders? Does he give the example of commitment to the Gospel?" In their discernment of suitable candidates for animator priests, they will look at the potential for leading others to the gospel and of themselves living the evangelical counsels and will not narrow this down to the question of marriage. They will not expect less spiritual commitment but even more. "Optional celibacy" has thus no meaning in this context either. It misleads everybody by focusing on the one aspect of celibacy.

The term "optional celibacy" is especially misleading for young candidates for priesthood. We believe there will also in future be young persons who wish to give their whole life for the service of the Church as priests. There will be options open to them, but these will be more than two and they will be different from those of yesterday. If a young person in future approaches the diocese with the wish to become a married provider-priest, the reply will be that there is no such option because the provider-priest will be phased out. If such a young person wants to become an OCL then the way is via very many years of proving oneself in daily life as a member of the Christian community. If the young candidate wants to become a member of a religious congregation/institute then there are of course the usual choices. Concerning the dioceses and their invitation to candidates to become animator priests, they will make sure to explain that the spiritual demands for becoming animator priests will become higher, not lower. Later we will come back to the question in which way dioceses can invite candidates for animator-priests.

It was the kind of semi-magic idea of the sacraments which has created much of the confusion and also led to the idea of "optional celibacy". That distorted view of the sacraments led many to ask as their first question: "How can I become a priest? What are the preconditions?" This should not be the first question. If it is, then it implies: "What conditions must I fulfill in order to be a priest? Must I be celibate?" Focusing only on the altar meant focusing on the conditions for getting to the altar. This led to the expectation that one day in the future there would be two kinds of access, two options. The access-to-the-altar approach will hopefully disappear, and in order to achieve this it is better to avoid using the phrase "optional celibacy".

* * *

In our efforts to clarify the above options of ordaining community leaders, especially with regard to option 3, the question will arise how this option compares with similar attempts made in the course of Church history, and with attempts made by some of the other Churches. Apparently there were some instances where something happened which might look similar to *viri probati* priests. We therefore have to ask ourselves whether we are perhaps in danger of repeating the failed models of the past, such as the thousands of uneducated priests of the middle ages? Are we possibly just reproducing the unfortunate model of the tens of thousands of village priests of the Ethiopian Orthodox Church? Are we heeding the lessons of history?

Learning from the successes and failures of history

In the middle ages we had too many priests and one of the aims of the Council of Trent was to reduce the incredibly high number; to have fewer priests and to have them properly trained in diocesan seminaries. Is option 3 repeating something that has proven not good? No, there is no comparison between the two models. The thousands of medieval "Mass-priests" existed because of an almost magic idea of Holy Mass, each priest celebrating alone on one of the countless altars in corners and niches of the Churches. The *viri probati* priests will conduct the liturgy together, always in a community celebration, always as a team, always with the collaboration of teams of lay leaders, and will be involved in much more than liturgy. They will not, like the medieval Mass-priests, live from Mass stipends but from their secular occupation. They will not appear as a clerical class. A low level of secular education or of theological training can constitute a danger but does not automatically do so. It was a danger for the mediaeval Mass-priest because it was coupled with a kind of magic understanding of the Sacraments about which the people had little understanding or knowledge. The *viri probati* priests' standard of education should be on a par with that of the people in the area; where that is of a low level, there will not be any problem because the community will probably change with the changing times and will admit more highly educated candidates when levels of education rise.

The same difference holds true for the village priests of the Ethiopian Orthodox Church. That Church is a shining example of indigenization but only in certain aspects. In other aspects it cannot be accepted as a model for our times as in the case of the type of village priests it has developed. These priests show the same characteristics as the mediaeval Mass-priests: low education, dependence on stipends, over-emphasis on rituals with strong magic inclinations among priests and people. Because everything focuses on ritual there is no critical community relationship which constantly challenges and questions leadership. The laity attends and watches the liturgy of the priests and has little active share in it. The liturgy is other-worldly with no intent to influence social change. There are lay officials but they are all related to the ritual.

The number of priests was incredibly high before the Ethiopian revolution of 1974. In 1971 the population is quoted as being 23 million, among whom 10 million were Orthodox Christians. There were 150,000 priests among them, one for every 60 people. Examples given are of villages with populations of 3,000 having 40 priests. A priest who administered Confession was supposed to hear the regular confessions of not more than seven of the faithful. He might have had his own land, but besides that he lived from stipends received for burials, confessions, blessings, and prayers. The result of this kind of village priests is that there is no lay involvement, there is a reluctance of the priests to relinquish office if this were indicated, and there is low esteem of these priests among the educated.[6]

Those who study the options envisaged for *viri probati* priests have also learnt from the historic development of the Protestant Churches. Option 1 is regarded as undesirable precisely because it comes close to the model of the pastors of the Protestant Churches. Those Churches wanted to abolish a clericalist type of pastors but, in spite of this intention, they have retained it. In recent times a few of them have pioneered in introducing a "tent-maker ministry" in order to overcome their clerical model of pastors, but this innovation is making only slow progress. To avoid the development of a clericalist type of *viri probati*, option 3 includes aspects such as the ordination of more than one leader per congregation.

From the models which have been successful in other Churches we can single out the Methodist Church. It is accepted that the Methodist practice of establishing teams of "preachers" in each small or large community has proved efficacious and has been adopted as the most suitable method by many other denominations in developing countries. According to this model, one full-time minister may serve an area of 20 to 50 kilometers in diameter with 50 or so congregations, each with five to ten "preachers." The interesting aspect is that the preachers rotate, for each Sunday service from congregation to congregation according to a "plan" which is decided and printed each year. This "plan" which has assumed strategic importance, assigns each preacher to a different congregation every Sunday. The preachers move to their assigned places at their own expense; their service is completely voluntary. The full-time minister visits each congregation only four times a year; on all other Sundays the local preachers together with the "scheduled" preacher conduct the service. The structure is held together by the regular meetings of all the preachers with the minister, by the strict procedure of appointing new preachers and by the

---

[6]   F. Heyer, Die Kirche Aethiopiens. Eine Bestandsaufnahme. Berlin / New York 1971.

need to be included in the "plan" in order to be accepted. This method has worked well over a long period of time, especially in developing countries.

Frequent celebration of the Eucharist is not seen as a value in the Methodist Church, at least not in the majority of the congregations. Therefore the training programme for preachers does not include the celebration of the Eucharist. It is not a matter of being unfit to conduct such a liturgy or being barred from it, but simply a matter of the particular theology the Church has adopted. The reliability of the structure, the low cost of maintaining it, and the fact that it has been copied by so many other denominations recommend it. If a Church with a high regard for the sacraments would adopt it, it would certainly be a promising model.

The Anglican Church has, at least in developing countries, copied the preacher model of the Methodists to a certain extent but over and above that, has introduced tent-maker priests and has done so not only because of emergencies but also out of much reflection how to overcome a clericalist model of priest. Anglican theologians such as Roland Allen have been spearheading the idea that the priesthood of the Church should not consist only of full-time workers and that the reasons for this are both practical and biblical. The Anglican Church has then started to introduce these self-supporting priests in various countries. Self-supporting priests continue following their secular occupation, are not trained in seminaries but, through correspondence courses and weekend seminars, are equipped to take charge of parishes. In the diocese which apparently has been the most successful with this scheme there are 160 priests of whom 130 are "community priests" and only 30 work as full-timers. [7]

The idea of not only ordaining *one* self-supporting priest but having a number of priests working as a team in a parish is to some extent known in the Anglican Church and is seen by some as an ideal, though hardly ever put into practice. This lack of the team principle has led to the fact that the self-supporting priests of the Anglican Church, although leading lay people's lives, make the impression of being clerics. They wear a clerical collar and try to be similar to the full-time priests. Many of the dio-

---

[7]   Figures of the Anglican Diocese of Pretoria, South Africa. Other Anglican Dioceses of Southern Africa also have high numbers of self-supporting priests, but it is sometimes only 40% of the total number of priests or a similar percentage.

ceses do not use the term "community priest" for them but rather speak of "self-supporting priests" and this reluctance to use new terminology may also be an indication that the original ideal is no longer the main motivation. Speaking of "self-supporting priests" one uses a financial definition whereas by speaking of "community priests" one emphasises a theological aspect.

We are of course aware that in the Anglican Church the obstacle against having a sufficient number of priests is not celibacy but finance. Anglican Dioceses are not only influenced by some of their theologians who urge them to move from clericalism to self-ministering communities. They are also influenced by the difficulty to find sufficient financial support for a full-time pastor in small, scattered parishes. Many dioceses opt for non-stipendiary, self-supporting priests because this is the only financially viable way to provide the smaller parishes with priests. Since this has now become the motivation, it is understandable that from both sides there are efforts to move back to the old clergy model: the self-supporting priests imitate the full-time priests as closely as possible, and the parishes try by all means to again get a "proper" priest. Both sides see the self-supporting priest merely as a substitute and want that substitute to resemble as closely as possible the real clergyman. Both sides see the self-supporting priests only as an interim measure which should end as soon as possible. In many places it is only some theologians and some bishops who focus on the original ideal.

This difficulty or even failure to uphold the original ideal of establishing self-ministering communities and of moving away from the clerical type of priests to "community priests" may serve as an important lesson. What starts as a search for an ideal may end in a pragmatic stop-gap measure. If one aims mainly at closing gaps, at finding a substitute for a missing provider-priest, then the ideal will evaporate. If one looks too much at the immediate practical emergency and too little at the target vision of the Church, the ideal can get lost.

We should certainly learn from the practices of other Churches but also from the good and bad experiences in our own Church, especially those made since the Second Vatican Council. There are innumerable publications describing the various ways, successful and otherwise, in which a sharing of ministry has been attempted. In our Catholic Church there is by now a wealth of experience on leading passive congregations towards a community life, on awareness raising and on animation, on inviting large numbers of voluntary co-workers, on the methods of offering training and formation on parish level, on combining faith-sharing with ministry training, on joint decision-making, on designing and planning local liturgies, on ways of safeguarding against monopolies and status seeking, on teamwork and on rotation of office, and finally on ways of helping the existing priests to become animators. Much of this experience has influenced this present study.

* * *

Now that option 3 has been described in various ways, we turn to a question which lies at its core, the question of our deepest reasons for seeking to introduce this new kind of ordinations: which are our real motives?

If we had tried to deal with this question at the very beginning, before looking at the proposed concrete options, this reflection on the motives might have become rather theoretical. We would have had to say again and again: "it all depends on the way this intention is implemented." By now we have seen the various practical suggestions and the main options available of us. The choice between them depends on our vision, on our deepest motives.

What are our deepest reasons for attempting to ordain *"viri probati"*?

The motives and reasons for introducing ordained community leaders

We have already seen that we need two kinds of vocations, the Paul-type of vocations and the Corinth-type vocations. The Paul-type is presently the only one existing and it is obvious that we will continue praying for it. We now ask ourselves for the deepest reasons why in our days we also need the second type which abounded in Corinth and all the early communities.

Most publications which call for the ordination of *viri probati* base their argumentation exclusively on the present shortage of priests. Only a few give us, in addition, other reasons which would at any time, even when there is no shortage of priests, motivate the ordaining of proven Christians. We offer below a few ideas on some additional and more profound reasons why some local proven leaders should receive ordination.

The shortage of priests: not the reason but the trigger

It is certainly true that it is the shortage of priests which has prompted us to examine the state of Church ministry. That shortage has given us the courage to rethink an age-old practice which seemed almost unquestionable. However, this trigger-motive is not to be confused with the deeper reasons why we should reintroduce the ordination of proven local leaders.

If the shortage of priests were the actual reason for ordaining community leaders, then we should discontinue the practice as soon as we have sufficient priests. If the arguments we present in publications and discussions for introducing the ordination of lay leaders mainly concern the shortage of priests, then we imply that the present policy is the totally correct one. This present policy excludes many charisms and admits only candidates who choose celibate, full-time priesthood and, as a consequence, we practically say that the communities cannot celebrate the Eucharist without the presence of a priest who comes from outside their ranks. This was never our explicit teaching or our intention, but our practice seems to give this impression. If we continue to place our emphasis only on the shortage of priests we re-enforce this wrong impression.

The present priest shortage has certainly been the trigger, the starter-motive, but it is neither the only nor the deepest reason for the ordination of community leaders.

Reasons for ordaining community leaders

It is actually wrong to put the question in this way: "Why should we ordain proven members of the community?" because it puts the onus of proof on the wrong foot. The proven community leaders are the more natural kind of candidates and it would therefore be more appropriate to ask "*why not* proven members of the community? Why restrict ordination to those who are not members of the local community, are not following an average profession, and do not have a family?" The onus of providing reasons lies with those who want to continue the present type of restrictions on the access to priesthood, not with those who want certain restrictions to be lifted.

It is also important to realize that *the nature of reasons* proffered is such that they are not intrinsically compelling, neither the nature of the reasons for the present restrictions nor of those for lifting them. We are not asking which choice for presidency *must* be made, but which is *more appropriate*, which is more suitable for expressing the meaning of the ecclesial community, of ecclesial leadership, and of the Eucharist in our times.

The motives or reasons we will now be describing arise from our present faith experience, from the way in which we, in these times, experience our faith. These reasons and motives are therefore a combination of our present sense of faith and our memory of the long tradition of the Church. They are born both out of reading the New Testament and out of our discerning the good aspirations of people of today.

A mature community should have its own presiders

The process of becoming a mature faith community includes many aspects, and one of these is that the community develops the ability to fulfill all its essential tasks by itself. An immature community is either unwilling or unable to do so, or prevented from doing it. The New Testament communities provide the model for a mature community. They were quickly enabled to assume all responsibilities even to presiding over their sacramental celebrations. However, they still welcomed and wanted the periodic visits of an apostle to ensure that their community life was complete and genuine.

The congregation which says: "We are able to do most things for ourselves, but for the authenticity of the Word and presiding over the sacraments we prefer to wait for somebody to be sent to us" cannot be considered as leading a complete or mature community life.

In recent years we have experienced an increased need to stress community building and self-reliance. Many efforts are being made to lead congregations from the stage of being provided for by outsiders to one of maturity. We should continue this evolution and guide the communities to that maturity where some of their own members can be ordained to preside over the proclamation of the Word and the celebration of the sacraments.

To show that it is *we* who celebrate, let our own leaders preside

A liturgical celebration is like a word the community is saying to God. God desires to hear the word of every community and each community wants to say its own word to God. It should not be someone who comes from another place who says the word on its behalf. For the word to be truly genuine, it should be uttered by the community itself. Of course this does not mean that the community's intention is to say this word in isolation but in communion with the Whole Church. This is why the situation must change and a community should have some of its own members ordained for the task of presiding over the celebrations. They will at the same time act as the link to the Universal Church.

In our days there is a felt need to move away from the passive, anonymous congregation to one where the members consciously come together, have a sense of belonging to one another, and act as a community. Therefore it is most fitting that the presiding ministers of the liturgical rites should be members of the celebrating community. In other words we should aim at some of its members being ordained for presiding over its own celebrations.

To show that God is everywhere in the world, let the people of the world stand at the altar

When we approach the altar, we bring ourselves to it with all we are. We should not say: "We cannot come to the altar because we are involved with the world of fields, of machines, of science, of families, of...", but instead: "We come to the altar with all we are". It is important for Christians to experience the whole world as being very near to God.

While this realization is necessary at any time, there is a renewed need for it in our times when so many people find it difficult to sense

God's presence in our modern world. Consequently it is important that some of those who normally preside over the sacraments live in the world in the same manner as the other members of the community. That is, some community members should be ordained for this service.

To show that we are a family, we must be allowed to assemble

Gathering for the family meal is fundamental to family life and this is also true for the new family of God's children. It is the task of every local congregation to assemble its members. Its sacred and sacrificial meal is the most essential sign by which it expresses in each place what it is. We must therefore do everything we can to enable each local community to celebrate the Eucharist as its own sacred sign of what it is: the new family of God's children.

Historical developments have brought us to a legal situation which in effect says: "You cannot gather without the presidency of a priest sent to you," but it is now time to return to the former principle that urged each local community to look for its presiders among the community members. Our renewed theology of the Eucharist as a sign prompts us to do likewise. The family should come together and the "elders" of the family should head the family table.

We should end the confusion of roles

It is harmful to continue with our present contradictory way of explaining that laity do not exercise official ministry when in fact they do, and that priests exercise all pastoral ministry when it is evident to everyone that lay people do most of it. Lay leaders who are able to express themselves clearly have made it known that they suffer under this lack of clarity. Their motivation is impaired because they feel they are asked to undertake Church tasks beyond their rights. This is particularly true of those who conduct a Service of the Word on Sundays or who practically bear a presiding responsibility for the whole community. Concerning other liturgical tasks, it is often only theologians who take note of the confusion, not the laity who conduct liturgies, preach homilies and lead communities; but this very unawareness of confusion is all the more reason to strive to resolve the dilemma.

People call many functions "lay ministry," which are actually something else, but we hesitate to use the correct terms, such as "presiding over the community" because we fear that we might lessen the status of the only existing kind of priesthood. Many Church leaders overreact by speaking of "clericalising the laity and laicising the clergy" while in fact the problem lies elsewhere. It is the result of not allowing the normal development of natural forms of pastoral ministries to take place.

Some priests see their role becoming ambiguous. They have to ask others to share duties which were exclusively theirs while officially stating that this should not be done.

Religious, too, feel the uncertainty. The shortage of diocesan priests forces them to act as diocesan priests; it becomes very difficult to explain their actual identity.

The ordination of proven local leaders will go a long way towards reducing the confusion. It will enable us to speak in an unambiguous way about communities, about priesthood, and about religious.[8]

We need sound motivations for full-time priesthood

In connection with the reasons given above for introducing OCLs, the Church has other needs as well. It needs clear motivation for those who want to become full-time priests. Motivation cannot avoid becoming confused and distorted when, as is the case in the present form of priesthood, all tasks and roles are expected from one person. We need more clarity.

There are numerous complaints that in spite of today's people-of-God theology taught in the seminaries a dominating kind of priest keeps on developing or re-appearing. The reason seems to lie in the fact that young candidates are formed by the atmosphere of the great shortage of provider-priests. They know that they will automatically hold a very special position among the people even if they have little to offer as spiritual wisdom and maturity. Whatever views they hold and whatever way they have of dealing with people, they are sure to be accepted as the only

---

[8]   Cf. the clarifications offered by P.Neuner in the chapter "Ministry in the Church: changing identity" in "Europe without Priests?" ed.by J. Kerkhofs, SCM 1995, 121-142.

existing spiritual providers. They know that they will be the only ones who can dispense the sacraments and this alone assures a kind of automatic superiority. It is unavoidable that this automatic superiority is experienced as a temptation to be less of a listener than a talker, to pay little attention to the spiritual situation of others but to adopt an attitude of knowing it all. The temptation to become a domineering person is too great to be avoided. The assurance of a monopoly is often stronger than our servant-theology.

The introduction of OCLs can be a powerful antidote against a monopolistic idea of priesthood. If parishes have teams of OCLs, young candidates for full-time priesthood will no longer aim at being the sole dispenser of sacraments. They will see that there is a constant and sufficient number of respected people who can administer the sacraments. In this context they will come to realize that the Church needs not only dispensers of sacraments but also priests who, above their liturgical role, are evangelisers, witnesses, spiritual friends, community builders, animators for the various charisms in a congregation, formators of the different kinds of ministers, and, in a special manner, are the link with the Universal Church.

The motive for becoming and for remaining a full-time priest will change when OCLs come into existence. Their presence among the people will change the expectations the communities have of a full-time priest. It will become a purifying factor for both priest and people. In other words, those who want to become priests are less likely to say: "What I want is to stand at the altar – never mind how," and the people less likely to say "What we want is somebody standing at the altar – never mind who."

The existence of OCLs will therefore be a powerful motive for priest candidates to make greater efforts to develop their ability to animate leaders and communities. At present many of them feel instinctively that even with little knowledge or skill their future position is unquestionable because nobody else can administer the sacraments. If OCLs become a reality and administer the sacraments, it will be immediately clear that something beyond that is expected of the theologically fully-trained priests. Candidates will take their formation more seriously because of the higher expectations they will have to meet.

Important reasons of the above nature are often overlooked. Those commonly given for the ordination of community leaders relate to the sacraments: the people must be "provided" with sacraments. If the traditional kind of priest is not available to "provide" them then we need additional "providers." This impoverished, distorted view of ordination and of the sacraments is not only a weak basis for the ordination of community leaders , but it perverts our whole evangelization. It should be replaced by the true conception of ordination.

We want to follow the self-ministering communities of the New Testament

Many New Testament scholars have reminded us that in the early years of the Church the one new priesthood was practised in slightly different forms in the various areas. None of those areas, however, would ever have dreamt of doing what we are practising today: telling the communities they could only celebrate the Eucharist when somebody who had been ordained somewhere else would be sent to them. The communities and the itinerant apostles automatically did the opposite. They ordained some of the local leaders so that the new communities could very soon celebrate the Eucharist on their own.

This practice was the only reasonable thing to do, also for practical reasons. For economic reasons it would have been impossible to have highly trained, Church-employed celebrators ordained and sent to each community. If the issue was discussed by those early communities, we can assume that they would have advanced not only practical reasons why each community should have its own ordained leaders. They would have advanced theological reasons. They would have pointed at their way of understanding the charisms given by the Spirit, the spiritual duty to use them and to accept them. They would have pointed at the nature of the Eucharist which was the thanksgiving of each community, not the thanksgiving of distant leaders.

If we try to sum up the theological reasoning of the communities of 2000 years ago in the terminology of today, we might find the modern term "self-ministering communities" most suitable to express what the New

Testament communities felt in their faith experience. They would have said, in their terminology, that the living Risen Christ wanted their communities to have some of their own leaders ordained for presiding over the Eucharist because He wanted their communities to be self-ministering communities.

If the New Testament communities had ever been confronted with the choice whether the celebration of the Eucharist should be reserved to the rare times when ordained leaders from outside could be present or whether these celebrations should be led by their own ordained leaders, if they had to choose between being ministered-from-outside and being self-ministering, their choice would have been clear and their reasoning as well.

For us, too, this term sums up in the shortest and most suitable way our reasons and motives for the proposal to introduce OCLs. The various reasons outlined above, are the thrust emanating from the faith experience of today inspired by the New Testament. They can be experienced and formulated in various ways, but if we try to sum them up in one term, then the term of "self-ministering communities" seems quite suitable.

Catch-phrases are useful to draw attention in summary form to the reasons for introducing OCLs. Up till now we have heard only the slogans "priest-shortage" and "the problem of celibacy". The catch-phrase "self-ministering communities" best focuses the attention on the above vision. Like all pithy sayings, it is open to misinterpretation. It could be misunderstood as the intention to build communities able to exist on their own, independently of the Universal Church. On the contrary, "self-ministering" has always been understood as placing the onus on a community to take as much responsibility as possible for itself but in communion with the other communities under the governance of the Universal Church. The value of the phrase lies in the forcefulness with which it expresses the main idea that God wants each group of believers to make full use of their charisms.

There is actually only one theological reason for introducing OCLs, our vision of Church. Some of its several components are outlined above. Those who cannot identify with this overall vision of the Church will also be against OCLs. Neither those who perceive the Church mainly as a powerful global institution nor those who regard it as a passive flock provided with spiritual care by a pastor coming from outside are likely to accept the idea of OCLs. Where they do cede to this novelty as being absolutely unavoidable, they see it only as an interim solution.

Those who follow the vision of the Church as a communion and for this reason also promote the idea of OCLs will try to communicate their vision in the most effective way and for this reason look for catch-phrases which pinpoint it.

Our theology of ministry: We want to be brothers and sisters in Christ's way

The deepest reason for introducing teams of OCLs is our theology of the Church and of its ministry. When we speak of a "theology of ministry" we do not mean a complete exposition of the essence of ministry in the Church or of the ministerial priesthood. We mean rather the particular theological emphasis which is the reason behind the suggested form the priestly ministry should take in our times.

One could have expected this study to begin with a theology of ministry and it may appear strange that a theological consideration is following only at this late stage. However, it was theological reflection which guided the reflection process throughout all the previous pages. In these first chapters options were evaluated, choices were made, motives for moving in a certain direction were described as they were experienced today. This was always done with a twofold perspective, one on the theological origin of the Church and its ministerial priesthood, the other on the "joy and hope, the grief and anguish of people of our time" (Vatican II, GS 1). This pattern was chosen because it leads to a more realistic kind of reflection. By allowing our lived theology of today to evolve the most relevant concrete forms, more attention is focused on these concrete forms and their feasibility.

Many theologians have shown in great detail how the concrete form of the priestly ministry has changed enormously throughout history. What a vast difference between a presbyter of the early Church and the priest of today. An elder of the early Church probably never in his life presided over the Eucharist because the bishop always fulfilled that role, while the role of the other elders was to stand next to him. An elder may have never baptized anyone nor administered any other sacrament because the presiding elder conducted those functions himself. During the whole week an elder was usually busy at his farm or in his workshop; only once a week would he stand at the altar next to the presiding bishop. How different from the priest of today who lives in a presbytery and whose main function is seen by most people as presiding every day at Holy Mass and to administer the sacraments.

Theologians have demonstrated that the norms by which the priestly ministry today is shaped must include both the teaching of Christ and the lessons taught by the tradition of the Church. We know that Christ sent the whole community of his believers to continue announcing and building the Reign of God and that this mission of the whole community is led, authenticated and crystallized in the work of those who are the pillars of the community. The mission of the whole community is one with the mission of those called to be their sacramental leaders. The mission can only be fulfilled together.

The ways in which these two aspects of the same mission are shaped and are interacting has changed to such an extent during the course of history that people of today would hardly recognise those forms as being essentially identical with forms of our times. Theology has also shown that these many stages of adapting the forms of Church life and ministry of the Church were not just accidental but were needed for the continuation of the work of Christ during the different historical situations. The lessons of history should not be regarded as something purely human, even though some changes were deviations from the gospel. The Church had to try to invent forms of priestly ministry suitable to each time. It had to adapt its ministry to times of persecution and to times of alliance with the state, to times of government chaos, to times of feudal systems and to times of powerful states. The same is our task today. The human failures and errors involved in this long process of adaptation should not obscure the fact that God taught us important lessons through the process, lessons which need to be respected even today.

We need to identify with the intention of Christ as he sent his Church and its leaders, identify also with the process through which Christ has guided it throughout history, and at the same time we need to identify with the genuine, God-oriented aspirations of people of today.

Listening carefully to these aspirations of today's believers we discern that the priority is the desire to become a community of brothers and sisters in Christ. The desire to be and to be seen as a community of equals has often been given the first place; this has also been acknowledged by the Second Vatican Council (GS 29 and LG 32). People want to be seen as equals and want to overcome anything that could indicate master-servant relationships. People of today are touched and inspired by the example of Christ who wanted to be a priest who is "like his brothers and sisters." (Hebr 2, 17)

Our sacramental ministry has to signify not only God as transcendent but also God as immanent. Some of our leaders should signify God as the one who is totally "other," and some as the one who is totally "with us."

The desire for participation and co-responsibility has also been acknowledged repeatedly by texts of the magisterium as a genuine aspiration of today's people. These terms were used as guiding concepts in the Puebla texts of CELAM in 1979 and became major headings in the encyclical *Christifideles Laici* of Pope John II in 1988.

In former times the believers may have felt called to be Church in different ways, and may therefore have been happy with different forms. But it is the task of today's Church to look for forms of priestly ministry which correspond to the signs of the times as expressed in the genuine aspirations of the believers and of all people of today. If bishops and theologians hear the genuine voices of the believers saying "we want to be brothers and sisters in Christ's way," then this is a theological norm for shaping Church life and ministry today.

We need to search for forms in which we can be Christ's community in such a way that we can be seen and experienced as brothers and sisters in Him. The ministry of the ordained will have to be shaped accordingly in such a way that both the community of believers and its ordained leaders fulfill Christ's mission together.

The suggestion to entrust the ordained ministry to a team of local leaders within the communities constitutes a major shift in the theological history of priesthood. It looks like a return to the practice of the first century but it differs in many ways from it. It was not conceived as a return to something practised before but rather as a response to the faith experience and the situation of today. The history of the first century of the Church was not the decisive motive, but more an enabling factor.

The theological history of ministry enables and urges us to respond in this way to the ministerial crisis and to the faith experience of today.

It is understood that in this process of designing our response, the misunderstandings and temptations which in our days could distort or contradict Christ's intention have to be avoided. If in our time the misunderstanding is prevalent that the authorization of the ordained ministry could be given by any local group of believers, then obviously concrete steps have to be taken to avoid such a misunderstanding. Any other similar danger or undervalued aspects have to be rectified through appropriate measures. If in our times people find it difficult to understand the value of permanent commitment and unending faithfulness, then the forms of Church life and of the ordained ministry have to guard against such danger. Such defensive measures are part of our task. These are, not the key motives, however, but are merely safeguarding actions. Whatever we see as normative in Christ's own way of exercising and shaping ministry must be a norm in our own effort to shape ministry today in the way that is needed for people of our times.

What was presented in the previous pages as the possible way in which the ordained ministry could be adapted to our times is based on this theological view of ministry. This theology of ministry will continue to guide our efforts to find ways of implementing the introduction of the ordination of teams of community leaders and of developing teams of animators for them.

* * *

We have now seen in several ways that it is not just a question of how we can **increase** the number of priests by ordaining some proven Christians. The question is **what kind** of ordained leaders we want to introduce. Introducing the wrong kind can be disastrous. We have taken time to consider details of various options. Having considered also the motives which should guide us and the theological basis for our efforts, we can turn now to the choice to make among the options before us.

A choice which is vital but could prove disastrous

Many people may point out that they fully realize the ideal type of *viri probati* among those outlined above to be option 3, ordaining teams of community leaders, but that they find this option too demanding and too great an innovation to start with. They might prefer to begin with a more accomodating type and later progress to the ideal one. Is this possible?

Is it possible to start with one option and later move to another one?

Let us begin with option 1. Can we begin by ordaining some employed Church workers and later move on to the ordination of teams of voluntary community leaders?

In this case each employed married priest is expected not only to solve the problem of the scarcity of the sacraments but also to work as animator. By a long process of animation the newly ordained married priest is to foster community spirit, develop a variety of ministries and, over a number of years, train teams of leaders. Thus he leads the whole community to a stage where it no longer needs the employed married priest, some of the leaders become as a small team to take over the priestly work in this community. The employed priest might then move on to another community to go through the same process. Is this a feasible plan?

From the experience gained so far in the field of community building, it is very doubtful that such a sequence of events could be expected. In developing countries, the Young Churches are well aware that remunerated jobs are very scarce and anybody holding any kind of employment clings to it for the sake of his family. Even where the job is poorly paid, it has to be defended. Would an employed or even partly-employed married priest make room for others? Would he train others to do what he alone can do and in this way make himself redundant? Would he accept a transfer to another place to begin the whole process anew? Would he be able and willing to animate and transform one or more communities and bring them to a stage where some of their leaders could be ordained?

The employed pastor-catechists in the Young Churches are a case in point. When dioceses want to reduce the number of their employed catechists in order to promote voluntary ministries, these paid catechists cannot be sent away or easily asked to look for different employment. They often resist the general animation of the whole community and the training of voluntary workers because this undermines the security of their own remunerated employment.

Another difficulty in the Young Churches is that of finding efficient animators among the employed catechists. Having animator-catechists is not a new idea; it has been practiced for more than twenty years. Since Vatican II many catechist-training centres have developed their syllabus with this in mind. The result, however, has not been encouraging. There are several reasons for this. One is that an animation-training programme is quite demanding and many candidates do not have the necessary talent to make it a success. A second obvious reason is that most catechists cherish the monopoly of their assignment and have no desire to become dispensable. A further important deterrent is the possibility of a transfer. This would create a difficulty for a person who has a family, especially in rural societies. We must also bear in mind that the animation processes needed after the ordination of OCLs will be even more demanding than the animation processes which pastor-catechists have conducted until now. The animation process necessary to prepare a community for the implementation of option 3 is a much more complicated process than what has been expected of catechists up to the present. If the majority of catechists in the Young Churches have shown so little success in the less challenging ministry, it is quite unlikely that they will succeed in animating their communities towards the more difficult aim of option 3.

As for the Older Churches and those in industrialized societies, one cannot presuppose that the highly paid "pastoral assistants," once they are ordained as *viri probati*, will be prepared to serve as animators of the community, to train a large number of voluntary workers and to form emergent leaders as teams of *viri probati* to administer the sacraments. They must surely realize that such a procedure will result in curtailing the number of employed married priests, thus jeopardizing their own office. They may therefore be unwilling to work towards achieving the goal of option 3. It is a frequent occurrence that the pastoral assistant with his family is placed in the parish house left empty by the priest shortage. If he were ordained he would remain there as full-time priest and become the kind of married pastor that has existed in the Protestant Churches over the last 400 years. Such Protestant pastors have to a large extent developed passive congregations similar to Catholic parishes, serving their Churches with a provider attitude similar to that found in the Catholic Church.

It will always be easy for these full-time pastors to find excuses why the animation process cannot succeed. In industrialized societies the majority of a congregation are intent on perpetuating the provider-type priest. If there is any possibility of continuing the status quo, this will be strongly favoured by them. So if *viri probati* are introduced as Church-employed priests, they will very probably continue the pattern of the provider-type of priesthood. It is most unlikely that they will guide the congregations to abandon that dated form of the Church to create a new form, a new vision.

Option 1 could therefore be seen as a kind of "palliative" for parishes, reducing the pain of the moment but hindering the process of growth towards becoming a Church of active communities. It would be a dead-end, at least for a long time. To begin with option 1 with the intention of proceeding later to option 3 could thus prove a disastrous course of action.

Is this also true of option 2 where there is one ordained *vir probatus* retaining his secular occupation and serving the community without any remuneration? A financial interest to avoid the sharing of his Church assignment does not exist in his case. Where this option will lead to in the future will all depend on the community consciousness of both the members of the community and the ordained person.

In some countries, especially in the Older Churches, a *vir probatus* may be chosen even though the majority of the parishioners take a passive role in that process. The congregation is interested only in finding some-body to provide the sacraments. One cannot expect that a congregation with this aim in mind will be motivated later to adopt option 3 and bring forth a team of *viri probati*. They would rather revert to option 1 and en-courage the part-time *vir probatus* to become a full-time priest.

With regard to the Younger Churches, where the community is already active and has a large number of trained leaders, what happens when one of them is ordained will depend entirely on the community-consciousness of the ordained person. The majority of the active community will later prob-ably want to change to option 3, but how will the existing *vir probatus* accept the idea to alter his position? It's a gamble – he might like the idea of sharing his office with others or, on the contrary, because he holds a unique position in the community and enjoys the new and special status which it affords him, he might try to block the development of teams.

Option 2 as ice-breaker before option 3?

The concern is genuine that the sudden introduction of *viri probati* teams, a major innovation, would be a shock to many and could lead to serious confusion in the Church. A preparatory phase of moderate change would prepare the faithful to accept and possibly even welcome option 3. Can either option 1 or option 2 serve as that stage if it is made clear that it is not the final option? We have seen that neither option when used as a stepping stone can proceed to option 3. Put into practice as entities, they cannot lead to a more comprehensive model, but can they not be used in a limited way and on a small scale as ice-breakers? An ice-breaker is not the freighter which carries the goods; it only opens the path and then remains behind while the real ship goes ahead to the intended destination. Can something of an analogous nature be done to introduce option 3? Cer-tainly the need exists; people have been so accustomed to the traditional forms of priesthood that they will find it too difficult to move straight into the best option.

There is a way it could be tried. The bishops' conference selects a few parishes in dioceses where pastoral planning is quite advanced. In those parishes one married, employed or self-supporting deacon is ordained priest. It is stated clearly that this is an initial stage of two or three years intended as a time of reflection on how to continue with the ordination of *viri probati*. No other diocese or parish may apply for the ordination of laymen until the trial period has expired and an evaluation concluded. There is a firm agreement between bishops and all others concerned that the pattern of one-person ordinations will not be continued. If the initial phase proves positive and there is the wish for an expanded service of *viri probati*, this will only take place according to option 3.

The limited use of options 1 and 2 would not cause any real chaos. It would prove specially helpful in countries where it is necessary to cushion the severe shock of introducing option 3. Needless to say, the best ground-work of preparing passive communities for eventually reaching option 3 is to take steps to implement the vision of Vatican II, through introducing many lay ministries, through many awareness programmes, through Small Christian Communities. It is the only way to prepare all three parties – pastors, communities and leaders – to see the need for and to accept option 3. The above suggestion is not a substitute for that vision, but an additional measure for preparing the way especially where people cling to traditions in the church.

Never again shall we decide without having clear options

Looking back now at the 1971 World Synod of Bishops and the high vote of 45% for the introduction of *viri probati*, we are amazed. Had the vote been slightly higher, would the bishops have been aware of the implications and of the irreversibility of such a decision? Did they realize that a new vision of Church was at stake?

The publications of that time concerning *viri probati* show little awareness of the different possibilities or of the many implications. It is unlikely that the bishops had more knowledge than what the publications provided. How could 45% vote for introducing a procedure they did not really understand?

One participant in the synod explained: "The outlines sent to the bishops before the synod to start discussions were not of very good quality, nor did they come in time for very wide consultation. The subject of the Ministerial Priesthood was discussed with varying depth by most bishops' conferences, and in many cases also by priests' gatherings, or was the subject of surveys…. The bishops therefore arrived in Rome very unevenly equipped, some with substantial studies, but many with rather confused results of indecisive conference meetings, and some with very little."

The same reporter also explains that the overall method of all synods made it unlikely to achieve clear results. He then goes on to list the reservations the bishops had against the ordination of *viri probati*: "The fact that to allow the ordination of married men anywhere would almost certainly cause reactions and pressures everywhere seemed to determine the stand of most. Some took the question a step further, to the level of authority. If some areas could have married priests, would those who wanted to retain a celibate priesthood retain the authority to do so? Others said it was an indirect and not altogether honest way of undermining celibacy throughout the Church. Nor did the likely position of married men who had been ordained priests seem a very satisfactory one against the background of a celibate clergy. It would surely lead to a second-class priesthood. Behind this lay other fears: the bishops could not foresee into what problems they and the church might fall. It would mean changes of administration, finance, pastoral methods, relationships between bishops and priests, and priests and laity. Would divorces and adulteries not be common in the present unsettled state of married life? It is a time of crisis in the faith and in the priesthood, so not a time to start such a change. Better to consolidate, hold on to tried forms, make do with fewer priests. Many thought lay ministries should be developed, and a diversity of supplementary ministries be brought into being by experimentation. This would also give the layman a better place in the church, though some warned that it might clericalize the upper layer of the laity and deprive the laity of their leaders." [10]

The fears were easy to formulate and the figures showing the shortage of priests readily available, but the proposed options for the introduction of *viri probati* were not clearly presented. It did not add up to a good basis on which to make a weighty decision.

---

[10] "The Synod assessed" by Oswin Magrath OP. AFER (Kenya) 1/72, 51-58. Quotations from 51, 53-54.

Possibly many bishops thought that the new kind of diversified priesthood should be allowed to evolve by itself in a natural way. The hope of this happening is a greater risk than that of the evolution of catechists or deacons.

Recently introduced ministries such as the well trained pastor-catechist, the lay ministries of lector and acolyte and the permanent diaconate have indeed evolved. They were unevenly established and accepted and were implemented in very different forms. In several places they were even allowed to lapse and disappear. The ministries of lector and acolyte have been under re-consideration for more than ten years and there is still no result. The permanent diaconate is a great success in some areas, in others less so. And yet, all this evolution and devolution has not really harmed the church; it has been a learning process. When the *viri probati* are introduced can a corresponding evolution be expected?

Priesthood has a more central place in the parishes than other ministries. Once *viri probati* are introduced in a certain form, the chance of changing this ministry is less than that pertaining to other ministries. While the non-priestly ministries function *next* to the focal role of the parish priest and do not hold the central place, the *viri probati* priests will hold that key place in the communities.

When it became clear that many employed pastor-catechists were hindering the progress of community building, it was difficult but still possible to overcome the opposition because the parish priest remained firmly in charge. It was more difficult when permanent deacons proved an obstacle to the community because their ordination had to be taken into account. But since they were not ordained to celebrate the Eucharist, parish priests could still find a solution, though it often took a long time and caused much pain in the communities.

With *viri probati* priests it will be much more difficult to rectify an unsuitable system. It is very important to make the right choice *before* introducing a certain model. Of course, even *viri probati* priesthood will and must evolve, but the implications are much more serious and therefore it is crucial to make a clear decision that it is only option 3 which will be implemented.

Reports on the Synod of 1971 are a good indication of how bishops will deliberate the matter of *viri probati* in the future. The fears and hesitations listed in the report quoted above are in the main still applicable today. However, developments over the last 25 years will have made an impact on all concerned. For those who want a community-based priesthood, the vision will be much clearer, its far-reaching implications more exact, the motivation surer and the determination stronger. On the side of those who feel the present setup should be maintained, it will be more obvious that a change of this kind is far reaching and irreversible. It will therefore be much more difficult to come to a decision. Whereas the report quoted above says there was a kind of euphoria in the Synod hall at that time, the atmosphere will be different when the next decision is due. What is needed before that is intense reflection and comprehensive clarification. The deficiently-informed vote of 1971 is an incentive to begin now, long before the next vote, to study all the possible options and what each implies.

Choosing the high road of ordaining teams of local leaders

For introducing the ordination of *viri probati* priests there is a low road which would mean ordaining here and there a good person who can preside over the sacraments. The high road is to ordain community leaders, but only after community building has succeeded and only as teams. The low road involves several serious dangers but seems to be easier to implement. The high road means ordaining only teams of local leaders, and only together with the simultaneous establishment of teams of animator priests.

The realization that the ordination of *viri probati* should not be attempted in an easy way but only in the more demanding way of teams is a key insight of our study. Easier models have been proposed by others. We have tried to understand them and have tried to envisage the consequences. The result has been that they lead to vastly different results, a fact that has surprisingly been overlooked by most people. Dangers have appeared before us of which most people are not aware.

Many will ask themselves why we should immediately choose the "high road" and not move forward in steps, trying something easier at first and only later attempting the higher ideal. In so many other areas of life, this has always been the more sensible way to attempt a change of this magnitude. The reply given in the above pages is that in this case it is harmful to initially try an easier solution. Our reply also says that this is an irreversible process. There is no later access to the high road in this case. The only access is the immediate one.

There are several things which make us hesitant to take the high road with regard to ordaining *viri probati*. We fear causing too much shock to all parts of the Church. We fear we might drive the conservative ones to such extreme rejection that they would rather break away from the unity of the Church. We fear we do not have the resources. We fear we ourselves might not yet understand the whole change involved. We do not feel confident to manage such an enormous step.

These fears are natural and realistic and we have to take them into account. Taking the high road does not, however, mean taking all steps at the same time. What it means is aiming from the beginning at this preferred model, and not at an easier one. The practical ways one can approach the ideal target model in manageable steps will be discussed in the next part.

One of our difficulties is that this high road is not open at all, or will not be open for a long time in certain areas of the church where the shortage of priests is severe. There could be several obstacles against this more demanding higher ideal of ordaining only teams. In some areas the communities are very small and only very few places would therefore be able to find a team of candidates. In other areas, relations between the priests or between the bishop and the priests are so difficult that a long-term approach of this kind is hardly feasible. Another obstacle could be that the dioceses of a country are unable to agree that any one diocese could go ahead with this approach.

In such circumstance, should one choose the low road? We have already seen that we can not start on the low road and then hope to move over to the high road. The message therefore seems to be clear: *viri probati* ordinations can only be attempted on the high road even if that excludes many areas in the beginning.

That message may be sad for parishes or dioceses who say they are not ready for the high road, yet have excellent individual candidates in some places. Many of those areas will understandably ask whether it is really not better to choose the low road.

Probably the answer to all those situations is to ask: which effective steps will you take to avoid making the low road the determining pattern? If effective steps can be put in place in a convincing way, this would become similar to what we called "ice breaker" solutions above. If, however, no convincing steps can be taken one has to ask which danger is greater: waiting – or risking the perpetuation of the low road? It seems clear that waiting for the high road is the safer option in these cases.

* * *

The expositions in Parts One and Two of this booklet lead to the conviction that the best choice among the various kinds of *viri probati* is option 3 of ordaining teams of local leaders. The question now arises how this option can be implemented stage by stage. Part Three will consider these practical steps. Option 3 is of value only if it can be implemented. The consideration of the steps of implementation are therefore an additional way of explaining and testing this option. In order to be consistent with the option we are taking we will, in this part, mainly use the term "ordained community leaders" (OCLs) instead of *"viri probati"*.

Those who have to decide whether it is feasible at all to introduce the ordination of community leaders are interested not only in the procedure of achieving this goal, but also in the implications this will probably have on many aspects of the church. It is therefore necessary to include chapters on ways of preventing too great a shock to the parishes involved and to the various sections of the church. The reaction of existing priests and seminarians, the effect on religious institutes and financial considerations are examined. How a structure of ordained community leaders could be sustained will be dealt with in some detail.

Part Three

How the church could begin ordaining community leaders

How to make the first move: by way of exceptions or how?

One could imagine various ways of introducing the ordination of community leaders (OCLs). Let us compare these.

Many are of the opinion that the highest authority of the Church, the pope and the bishops, should simply decide to allow all dioceses to introduce ordinations of this kind. This may appear the easiest approach, but one not likely to be chosen at this time. It is not even probable that a general permission would have been given in 1971 when the vote of the Synod of Bishops almost favoured the introduction of *viri probati*. Today, many years later, the bishops themselves are more reluctant because they are more aware, though only in a vague way, of the enormous change this step would cause in the ministry structure of the Church. They also fear that it could cause serious disunity in the Church.

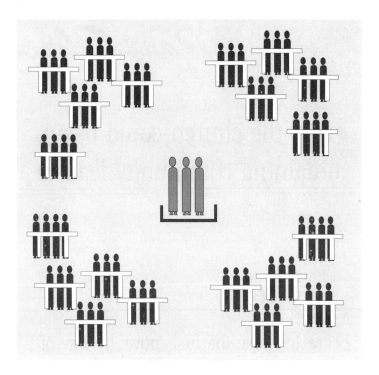

A general permission would cause severe shock throughout the Church. A large number of parishes would find themselves completely unprepared. Many bishops and priests would not be ready to cope with the change and might make irremediable mistakes. People will assume that the universal celibacy of priests is soon to be abandoned. There would be fierce opposition from the conservatives in the Church to the point that they would undertake militant action which could threaten the unity of the Church. It would create consternation in the seminaries and could cause disruption there. Women may react strongly at being excluded and decide that now or never is the decisive moment for them to demand ordination. A general permission is neither acceptable nor workable.

There are other possibilities. One is that not all but only certain selected countries are given this permission. The advantage of this kind of approach is that a whole episcopal conference can cooperate in designing the best process step by step so that hasty or unprepared ordinations and other mistakes can be avoided. It would be particularly helpful if a whole country would design and conduct dialogue sessions in order to make sure that proponents and opponents can voice their opinions and nobody feels bypassed. If the intention is to move to a more community oriented Church, then this mode has to be practised during the stage of deliberations, long before the first ordinations of community leaders. However, this country-based permission may still be considered too risky to initiate, and quite possibly there are very few countries where the episcopal conference is so united that the bishops can jointly introduce such ordinations.

The situations of the Older and Younger Churches differ considerably. In the latter the shortage of priests is greater by far, and these Churches should be the first to be given permission to ordain lay leaders. Although they are more ready for it than the Older Churches it is unlikely that they will be the first to ask. There are several reasons for this. The Catholic media in the Young Churches is comparably weaker and public opinion not so powerful. The parishes and communities are much more active but they do not voice their pressing need for a new kind of priests. They suffer in silence without demanding a solution. Their bishops realize the difficulties connected with such an enormous change and prefer the Older Churches to make the start. We look at their reasons later.

There would indeed be great advantages if a whole country first conducted a dialogue and then made a joint decision to ordain community leaders. The clarity achieved would make it easier to face the threatening question: "where will this lead us?". It will also prevent some from taking the law into their own hands, which could happen where the way ahead is not clear. To conduct dialogue would be an advantage, although we know that dialogue necessarily causes some tension. The danger is not dialogue itself, but magnitude of change caused by a whole country moving ahead at the same time. In today's volatile Church, there is the danger of disunity and even of a split if a start is made which involves the whole Church or a whole country. Therefore we have to resort to less dramatic strategies.

The most promising approach would seem to be by way of exception. It, too, has its disadvantages which we will review later, but this type of procedure seems to be the least threatening one. Its chief asset is in reducing the shock of change. It gives more time to adjust to this innovation. It allows the hesitant parts of the Church to observe how the initial attempts succeed. It gives everybody the opportunity to learn from mistakes.

To begin with, it is necessary to realize that exceptions can be understood in different ways and can take several forms. We will compare these.

Which way of making exceptions?

When we speak of ordaining community leaders by way of exception we mean that certain dioceses will ask the highest authority in the Church for permission to ordain a limited number of proven community leaders. When making their request, they do not think of a change in Canon Law with its requirement of celibacy for the ordination to priesthood. They ask for an exceptional permission which does not question the existing law of universal celibacy.

Let us now reflect on whether this procedure is feasible, what its most likely implications are, and what practical tasks would be required for implementing it. These first moves to introduce ordained community leaders could take different forms and cause different reactions. Here are some possibilities:

Exceptions which avoid all publicity.

This means that a small number of dioceses suffering from a severe shortage of priests could quietly obtain from Rome the permission to ordain a very small number, from 1% to 5% of the permanent deacons in a country where there are many hundreds of them. There is no public announcement, no previous debate in the council of priests or the diocesan pastoral council. It all happens in a rather inconspicuous way.

The communities concerned are not shocked at all as they have become used over a long period to the liturgical presence of the married deacons. The country as a whole eventually comes to hear of these rare exceptions and this triggers off a series of discussions among the various sectors of the Church, including the other deacons and lay leaders. It doesn't, however, cause a storm, because the exceptions have been granted to a restricted extent and will not easily be expanded. The conviction can be maintained that this is an experimental step, not yet the beginning of a landslide.

This quiet, almost stealthy method has the advantage of avoiding public commotion but has the disadvantage of all decisions having to be made without consulting the congregations. It ignores the need for community building and it could, in a new guise, perpetuate the old model, the providing Church.

Exceptions preceded by public dialogue

Every family knows that there are different kinds of exceptions. Some demand by their nature that they remain almost unknown. Even if they become known to some, everybody avoids making them an issue of the whole family. There are other exceptions which, again by their nature, demand that they be treated differently. They should be known. Although it is only one or two who are granted an exception, others should know about it, should understand why it was granted, why only to some and not to all, and what would happen next. The family senses that a public debate of the whole family is better than some rumours circulating or some private discussions between the family head and each one concerned. It is healthier for family relations that this kind of exception be dealt with publicly. The easy acceptance of the next step in the family will be more secure, either the refusal of the next request for an exception, or the multiplication of the exception, or the lifting of the old rules, whatever may follow. Any of these future moves will proceed in a better family atmosphere if this second kind of exception was discussed freely.

Dioceses could follow this second path by discussing publicly the idea of ordaining a small number of community leaders. The process demands extensive involvement with congregations and the courage to face opposition. It entails taking risks, but would prepare everybody in a much better way for the new vision of Church.

The dialogic approach is advisable everywhere but especially where a repeated public demand triggers the whole process. Since this demand is coupled with the call for a more participative type of Church, the bishops will not wish to make this decision alone, without the various councils and without the people.

An additional motive for using a public method is the fact that in some dioceses of the Older Churches there is no proper foundation for OCLs. Most parishes have made little progress in community building, and in the development of shared ministries. Dialogue meetings would motivate the parishes to accelerate the processes of community building. It would show many of them that this is the only way to move beyond the problem of a shortage of "provider priests."

Furthermore, in these dioceses there may be people who are too eager to be ordained. This could happen where there is a large number of theologically fully-trained people, some of whom regard themselves as the obvious candidates for ordination although they have not emerged as leaders from the congregations among whom they live and for whom they are already employed full-time by the diocese. If there is no dialogue with the priests, with the pastoral workers and the communities, then such "obvious candidates" will appear as the only possibility. There may be many local charisms but there has never been a chance to discover them. Great harm can be done if in this way the whole process is limited to these candidates while the possible local leaders are bypassed. The whole parish must realize that a process of several years is needed before it can meaningfully begin to consider introducing OCLs and find the candidates who can truly form one community with the people.

The need for public dialogue becomes apparent if we remember that a large part of the Church actually want something wrong when they speak of *viri probati*. They are thinking of additional providers, anybody who can administer the sacraments. Their demand is a desire to perpetuate the provider-type of Church life by introducing a new and additional kind of ordained providers. Their outlook contrasts sharply with those who see the move towards ordained community leaders as a historic chance to make a great leap forward by bringing about a new vision of a communitarian type of Church life. There is certainly a great need for awareness of the difference between these two ways of viewing the *viri probati* question, and this will happen only by way of open dialogue.

The invitation to public dialogue meetings should, according to circumstances, state whether the decisions reached still depend on the consent of certain Church authorities (the bishops' conference, Rome). It is necessary also to stress that the discussion is to be limited to the possible introduction of only a very small number of OCLs.

During public dialogue meetings three posters can be displayed, representing the three choices which lie ahead of us, and making us aware of the enormous implications of each:

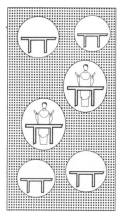 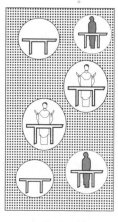 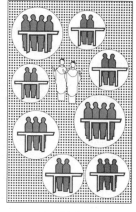

A	B	C
Continuing as at present, where many of the communities have no priest. The sacraments remain infrequent. People lose the sacramental sense.	Ordaining one person in a community which has no resident priest, in order to make the sacraments more available.	Ordaining a team of local proven leaders in each community; the full-time priests become the "animators" or "coordinators" of the many ordained leaders.

The purpose of the dialogue meetings will be:

1. to distinguish between different types of OCLs (teams or individuals, voluntary or employed, emerging or appointed, working with or without other active lay leaders);

2. to discern the diverse implications of each type of OCL for the life of a community, for the present priests, and for the whole Church;

3. to understand the reasons why others are opposed to the introduction of OCLs;

4. to realize that when parishes think about asking permission to introduce OCLs, they begin not by looking for possible candidates but by a lengthy process of preparation for the congregations and the priests; and

5. to possibly begin building up a broad backing of the project.

Resource material for this kind of dialogue could be the statistics of the particular diocese and the pastoral plan, also graphic diagrams such as those depicted in this booklet and a "list of preconditions," a sample of which is offered in a later chapter (pp. 148-150).

The dialogic process cannot be limited to one meeting; it requires a series of meetings. It should take place not only in the few parishes where most probably a team of OCLs will first be introduced, but also in other parishes to give many Catholics the opportunity to discuss this important issue freely. It is important for people to know what is happening in the Church so they feel part of it.

A discussion meeting is always more successful when conducted by a team, not by one person. The team should include priests and lay people, and as far as possible consist of local people. Dioceses would have to prepare a great number of local parish teams to conduct a series of dialogue sessions in as many places as possible.

What reactions can be expected as the outcome of the public meetings?

One fruitful result will be the realization that the question of OCLs cannot be solved properly by a sudden decision of Rome. Many parishes will become aware of how unprepared they are for introducing OCLs. People will understand that it would be unwise to begin immediately with the ordination of large numbers of community leaders, that the start should be made by way of exceptions where the need is great and where the congregations are ready to accept the change. The importance of community building and the sharing of ministries will come to the fore, so that even where the introduction of OCLs is not within reach parishes will be motivated to become more communitarian oriented.

The idea of ordaining community leaders in a few exceptional cases will be well publicized in the local and in the international press. However, the statements that only a very small number of OCLs can be considered at this stage and that there are preconditions which only few parishes can meet will lessen the impact. Mostly it will be a wait-and-see reaction while at the same time a healthy process of conscientization will begin. The small-scale beginning will forestall any fear that the existing discipline is abandoned and priestly celibacy would be abolished forever. (The next chapter comments on the probable reactions of various people.)

A public dialogue before asking Rome?

Can neighbouring bishops in one or more areas agree to set the dialogue in motion before asking Rome for permission? To ask for and wait for permission to conduct dialogue before beginning any discussion on the topic may entail a long delay. In the meantime, unrealistic ideas about *viri probati* continue to cause bitterness among the people.

Especially where there is a public and repeated call for the ordination of *viri probati*, it does not appear to be disloyal if dioceses decide to conduct public dialogue and study meetings. It would be stated that the purpose of the meetings is to get more clarity about the already existing public demand, ever strongly voiced but presented in so many confused ways. Some forms of the demand are unrealistic; it would therefore defuse the situation if people themselves come to realize this.

A public dialogue which begins in Rome?

This is another possibility. Could a group of dioceses ask Rome for conditional permission to ordain a limited number of community leaders, the condition being that dialogue meetings will be held and will produce sufficient clarity. The dioceses undertake to conduct the dialogue in such a way that it gives opponents a chance to voice their views. Only if it leads to an agreement on a meaningful type of OCLs by a high level of consensus will the outcome be presented to Rome for final approval. Another possible precondition could be that after the dialogue sessions the bishops' conference agrees by a fairly high majority to make the request to Rome.

The above examples of various types of public dialogue could be modified in many ways. Much will depend on the mood of the times and on the willingness of the various partners to conduct dialogue.

Why so much stress on dialogue?

Some may question the need for so much dialogue. They may compare the exceptional OCLs to other, seemingly similar, exceptions which have been granted in several countries in the past, such as the acceptance of married clergy of other Churches. Their ordination did not cause any shock nor did it cause any division in the Church. There were no dialogue sessions and yet there was no dissatisfaction. The difference is, however, that those were exceptions which hardly anybody could follow. It will be quite different with the first exceptional cases of OCLs, a phenomenon which everybody will understand as the beginning of a trend that could multiply in the Church. Once the first few exceptions are made, everybody will realize that there are thousands who could follow suit. In the case of the ordination of the few married clergy coming from other Churches everybody knew that only very few would ask for ordination in the Catholic Church.

The existing priests did not feel insecure because of the appearance of the few married priests who were former clergy of other Churches. Many of the priests and seminarians will, however, be deeply disturbed by the first exceptional OCLs. The celibacy debate has been simmering continually in the Church and has escalated over the last 50 years. It was not really affected by the exceptions made on behalf of the few married Protestant ministers, but it will flare up again when exceptions are made to ordain married leaders. The news of the possible ordination of some married viri probati can be understood as meaning "ordaining the first handful of thousands who could follow." Everybody will know that it does not mean "ordaining a handful whom hardly anybody could follow." To avoid undue confusion and bitterness it is wise to dialogue on the possibility of OCLs and to do so in good time.

It will become apparent in these pages that a broad backing is needed for introducing a change of this magnitude. The new ideas open the door to many misunderstandings and to many painful accusations. There must be more than a few individual Church leaders who can discuss these possible innovations and who stand for the high road which the Church is taking by changing its priestly ministry in this way. There must be broad backing for this change, and broad conviction that this is the right road to take.

The dominant Church atmosphere of a particular country is another important factor for considering the feasibility of introducing the ordination of community leaders. In some countries there is a prevailing mood of tension in the Church. The hierarchy is being criticized at every opportunity; bishops appear rather isolated from the communities, and there are well organized groups of militant conservative Catholics. The introduction of OCLs will cause serious reactions there, very different from the way it will be received in countries where the whole situation of the Church is quite the opposite. In considering the likely implications of ordaining some OCLs, these differences must be kept in mind.

Initial reactions to the news that community leaders may be ordained

The reaction of the average practising Catholic

Several surveys have been made of the most likely reaction of the average practising Catholic. The results repeatedly show that a substantial majority are in favour of the introduction of OCLs. Most of the very active Catholics will gladly welcome the move; others will take part in discussions and support will increase.

Among the less involved Catholics we can foresee that there will be a majority for OCLs, although they may support it for reasons which are based on much ignorance. Those who are not active in the Church but for some reason are hesitant about change in the priesthood will probably find it not worthwhile to argue about it. Some of them may be against *viri probati* because they fear they may not be well provided with the services of the Church, but since they are distanced from the active life of the

Church they are not even interested in opposing the introduction of the new priests. The main opposition will come from the militant conservative individuals and groups whose reaction we will consider later.

The reaction of the priests

All priests will realize the importance of the granting of these exceptions but the likelihood of in-depth discussions will depend on the attitude of the particular diocesan leadership.

Dioceses which are in principle against OCLs will say that there should be no change. The topic will hardly be discussed.

It will be different in dioceses which are in favour. They will convene many dialogue meetings, especially with the priests, and they will be eager to discuss the whole issue at great length. The realization that they themselves are being called upon to assist in bringing this new vision to reality will intensify their interest. It is not only one new kind of priest which is to be instituted, there will be two new kinds of priest which means that their priesthood will change to some extent, not in essentials but in practice. They will be deeply concerned to define their new role.

The priests who are not involved in the introduction of OCLs will react less vibrantly and will adopt a wait-and-see attitude. They will note that the decree lays down restrictions, especially concerning the number of exceptions, and will note the exhortations to all existing priests to remain faithful. The publication will create some uncertainty. The actual ordination of the first OCLs will still be several years away. The main factor for reassuring many of the existing priests will be that a new and important role is waiting for them.

For these reasons we can assume that in the early stage not much will happen among the existing priests and there will be no wave of defections.

The reaction of candidates for the priesthood in seminaries

When the candidates for the priesthood hear about the exceptions concerning the ordination of married leaders they will demand to know what they can expect. They should be informed about the vision underlying these changes, the new role of the animator priests, and the possibility that a religious community of diocesan priests will be established.

The majority will probably continue with their formation, and only very few will withdraw from the seminary because they feel unable to make a commitment to celibacy while married community leaders are being granted the permission to be ordained. A small minority may decide not to continue with their preparation for the priesthood in a Church which they think is about to abandon the universal celibacy of priests. One or the other might leave because of the exceptions and prefer to join the OCLs ten or twenty years later.

The resolve of the students to become celibate priests could weaken if they are not properly counseled on the meaningfulness of celibacy in making a deep commitment with the sacrifice of one's life. Some may have a simplistic theology of celibacy as if priesthood itself was incompatible with marriage. This needs to be rectified.

There will be confusion among students in a country which shares one common seminary. If some dioceses ordain community leaders while others do not, tensions will be felt in the seminary. Open dialogue and transparency regarding all the aspects of introducing OCLs are the only ways of preventing unnecessary tensions.

The reaction of women's liberation movements

Although the initial exceptional ordinations of community leaders will be few, women will soon ask why only proven men and not proven women are admitted. This could become a very strong confrontation, and could lead to a situation where many good Catholics will call for a halt to the whole experiment until that question is resolved. When dioceses begin pleading for exceptions to be increased, women will become more strident in their demand not to be left out.

Women will rightly point out that among the "proven" members of the Christian community women are certainly the majority. Once we introduce the criteria of "proven" it becomes almost ridiculous to speak only of "viri." It is too obvious that almost every group which discusses this question will ask why women should not be considered as proven local leaders.

The question will of course arise with different intensity according to the local cultural situation. However, even in cultures where leadership of women in society was inconceivable only a few years ago, things are changing. In African parishes it all depends whether women have found equal access to education and whether social mobility has set in. Where this is the case, women are today accepted as leaders of Sunday liturgies and even of funerals. Funerals are often more important and more sacred to African Christians than the sacraments and yet women are more and more accepted as funeral leaders while a few years ago they had to stand a long distance from the grave so as not even to get a glimpse of the carefully wrapped corpse. Soon it will be a third of the population of Africa who live in cities and this will include women to a great extent in the leadership structure of the parishes. It is, however, true that women do not yet insist on their equality with the same intensity as they do in industrialised societies. Once the question of OCLs is raised, the issue of the inclusion of women will be raised almost everywhere, though with different intensity.

For the proponents of the inclusion of women among the OCLs, two aspects will militate against each other. On the one hand it will appear to them that this is the best moment to demand equality and therefore inclusion among the OCLs. On the other hand it will also be clear that this might be counter-productive.

Quite a few women have said that one should first abandon the clerical image of priesthood and only then would women want to be priests. The possible introduction of OCLs will do just that. It will change the image of priesthood. It will gradually replace a clerical kind of priests with a community-based model. This would make the ordination of women much more attractive to many women and more acceptable to men. The number of women supporting their inclusion among the ordained will greatly increase if the parishes already have OCLs. To delay this step by opposing it at this initial stage would therefore be counter-productive.

At the same time there will be many who understand that OCLs can only be introduced in an organic way and this would mean to follow a certain list of preconditions, similar to those listed in a later chapter. Among those preconditions must surely be a sound diaconate, well proven over a number of years. The first hurdle to be taken must therefore surely be the inclusion of women in the diaconate, a question which is open to debate in the Church. Many will agree that this is the point on which one should focus at this moment.

Parishes and the Church authorities will be engaged in intense dialogue on those questions. They will probably come to the conclusion that the ordination of some community leaders is a tentative, experimental step. We can at this initial stage not yet say how it will end, and we cannot even give final answers to seminarians and to priests, still less to women. We therefore have to ask each of these groups to understand the impossibility of solving all their questions now. We must move step by step and are unable to say how the institution of OCLs will develop. The most we can do is to promise that we will, after a certain number of years, conduct another round of dialogue with all sectors of the Church on the results of the first years and on the next steps to be taken.

The reaction of militant conservatives

Militant conservatives will react forcefully. They have strongly opposed the changes in the Church since the Second Vatican Council. The announcement of a possible change in the ordained ministry will be alarming for them. The more they realize that it is not just a temporary emergency solution which is envisaged but a new image of the local community, the more they will agitate for refusal of permission to initiate OCLs. They will insist on being told to what limit the ordinations will be allowed and whether the universal celibacy of all full-time priests will remain perpetually in force. Some will demand that certain dioceses never be touched by these innovations and say they will withdraw from parishes which have *viri probati*, as they could not receive the sacraments from married priests. They may also threaten to find their own traditional priests.

However, these threats will most probably remain conditional "if the Church dares to abolish celibacy..." and will not be carried out immediately because officially there is no change in policy – the few cases of change remain an exception to the rule which is officially retained.

The reaction of Young Churches

Young Churches may not show the enthusiasm for OCLs which many are expecting of them, and it is important not to misunderstand their reaction. It is not a convinced, final, irreversible rejection but a hesitation before the unknown and at the same time a refusal to be rushed into foreign plans.

a. Young Churches hoping for speedy indigenization

A good number of dioceses in developing countries will find themselves in a dilemma when the announcement is made that it is now possible to ask for the exceptional introduction of OCLs. On the one hand they suffer from a severe shortage of priests and find it difficult to ensure a proper sacramental life for the young communities. On the other hand they are half way through the process of replacing the missionaries with an indigenous clergy and are busy establishing the image of the indigenous priest. The communities and their local priests need some time to forget the image of the missionary priests and to replace it with one more germane to their own culture. This is a lengthy and far-reaching process. It embraces many other components as well. There is the issue of status and power, the issue of cooperative relationship with the community, the question of finance, and many questions about culture. The transition is creating a certain division in the parishes between the older people who keep on comparing the local priests unfavourably with the missionaries. At the same time the indigenous priests are struggling with many enigmas in trying to establish a good and realistic pattern of indigenous priesthood on a par with the model set by the missionary priests, even if they wish to differ to some extent from them.

The bishops are deeply involved in this process of transition and encourage all concerned to make it a success. They continually address the communities, the seminarians, the young priests, the missionaries in order to establish the new idea of a local Church with a local clergy. Not everything can be expected to go well in the evolution from a missionary to a local Church. The bishops find themselves faced by doubts, confusion, suspicion, despair and even accusations. In this problematic situation it is almost impossible for them to be positive about ordaining local leaders.

The indigenous priests will influence the judgment of the bishops. In many Third World countries ordination to the priesthood is seen more as being entrusted with a cultic role than with an evangelising one, and this in spite of all the theological definitions. The indigenous priest feels he is special because of his cultic role, being the only one of his kind far and wide. He will therefore see it as a threat even to discuss whether some community leaders could be ordained. The possibility threatens to rob him of his special place. Although the bishops may realize that this attitude has little in common with the Gospel, they are aware how strong the priests' feelings are about protecting their role in the community and they prefer not to challenge their reaction. In many cases they would gladly welcome ordained community leaders to alleviate the shortage of priests but are afraid that this would add to the confusion during the difficult period of transition to a local Church with its own local clergy. This causes a dilemma for the bishops. Their response to the revolutionary new concept of a diversified priesthood is that it should first be tried out by others, especially the Older Churches, before being considered in the Young Churches.

Some of the Young Churches are experiencing a rapid growth in the number of Christians and of indigenous clergy, and a spirit of expectancy prevails, often even beyond realistic possibilities. The fast pace of development is accelerated especially by the growing percentage of indigenous priests whose influence in the presbyterium is constantly increasing. One hurdle after another is taken and there is an atmosphere of hope that the establishment of a truly local Church of the traditional model is achievable in the near future.

There may sometimes be a difference of opinion among the clergy. Where there is still a majority of missionaries, the ordination of community leaders will meet with approval; they feel strongly about the shocking unavailability of the sacraments in the majority of communities. At the same time the indigenous clergy fear that the newly emerging concept of a local clergy will be endangered by this innovation.

A wait-and-see stand seems justifiable and should not be interpreted as a total rejection. If the bishops of Africa presently say NO to OCLs, it does not mean that they want the Church as a whole to refrain for their sake from taking the step. It means a NO for the present for Africa. What will be suitable for them in the future, they reserve the right to decide at the proper time.

b. Young Churches beyond the stage of rapid growth

Some Young Churches have passed beyond the stage of rapid growth and a different reaction can be expected from them. They have a good percentage of indigenous priests and an indigenous bishop, but they realize that for a long time to come they will have to beg for some additional expatriate personnel. They are concerned that the very rare celebration of the sacraments will endanger their work of deepening evangelization among the faithful and they see the need of supplementary forms of ministry. Their original irrational expectations have given way to more attainable aspirations. The people and the bishop might love to have a completely indigenous clergy of the traditional kind, but it has become clear to them that this ideal will not be achieved by refusing a diversity in the priesthood. Their priority will shift to the deepening of evangelization, and the daring innovation of ordaining community leaders may appear as a realistic way of achieving this.

An indication of such a possible variety of reactions was the rejection of the permanent diaconate. This occurred in 1970 when the relatively young and rapidly growing AMECEA dioceses met in Lusaka. The theme of their meeting was "The Priest in Africa Today." They rejected the diaconate because they were convinced that the introduction of the permanent diaconate would compromise the present model of priest. The much older Latin American dioceses, too, rejected it, but for the opposite reason; they wanted a new kind of *viri probati* priest, not the diaconate.

The reaction of Young Churches may appear strange. Many of them are better prepared than the Older Churches for introducing community-based ordinations and they would need them more urgently. Yet they make the demand less forcefully and are more prepared to continue suffering under an unsuitable traditional pattern of ministry.

There is a diversity among the Young Churches. Most Churches in Africa are at the stage of rapid growth while in Latin America the majority have passed the stage of rapid growth. Young Churches in Asia may belong to either of the two but their particular local culture has to be taken into account. Some of their countries have a very high regard for celibate religious leaders and for this reason will be loath to consider the ordination of community leaders at present or in the foreseeable future. They will, however, be aware that their situation is quite exceptional. Their interest will be geared to preserving the traditional form of priesthood in their area and in keeping with their culture rather than in preventing the introduction of OCLs in other countries.

One must be careful in interpreting some of the documentation available. Developments are progressing very fast in the Young Churches. What was stated a few years ago is no longer held and opinions may change just as quickly tomorrow.

In the early 70s there were several small surveys or resolutions of priests' meetings in parts of Africa where the priests supported the idea of ordaining *viri probati* priests. Today one hears practically nothing about this idea in Africa and there are even voices which strongly reject it. When 25 bishops of West and Central Africa made the same request in an official way at that time, they were mainly expatriates and their present locally born successors are almost unanimous in rejecting that idea.

It is understandable that many leaders of Young Churches feel like the Lusaka meeting of the East African bishops which said their dioceses "should not become the testing ground for European experimentation and that the Africa Church should be entitled to solve its own problems in its own way and with its own speed".[11]

---

[11] Reported in SHARING (Gaba, Uganda) 2/1970, p. 7.

In other parts of the developing world the Young Churches show similar signs of a rapid change of view on this subject. The change partly reflects the transition from expatriate missionaries to locally born clergy, partly it is caused by a sudden increase in vocations in the respective areas. Situations change quickly, views have changed rapidly and can change again. In many areas of the developing world this is not the time to ask the Young Churches for a considered, long-term view on this subject.

At the same time it is a fact that the Young Churches will be deeply influenced by the way the Older Churches are developing the structure of the Churches ministry. If the Older Churches introduce the ordination of *viri probati* in a way which is not community orientated, the Young Churches will eventually suffer through this deplorable step. Their present parish life was shaped by the way ministry had historically developed in Europe and although they will increasingly be able to take more responsibility for their own development they will still be greatly influenced by what is happening now in the Older Churches. The fact that many of the Young Churches can at this moment not be expected to present their final view on this difficult question cannot mean that they wish all reflection on this subject to be shelved. It is vitally important for them that sound reflection be undertaken on the best way of developing the sharing of ministry.

* * *

In this chapter we have considered the most likely general reactions of various sections of the Church to the decision that in some areas a number of exceptional ordinations of local leaders may take place. We will now turn to the specific reaction of the group which will be most affected by this decision, the existing priests of those areas where the start is made. Their traditional role will be most affected.

A new role for existing priests

In the areas of the Church which decide to introduce *viri probati* under certain conditions, there will be many meetings in which priests, theologians and bishops reflect on the way this development will influence their own role.

This period of discernment might be lengthy and should not be hastily curtailed. If the time taken becomes an issue and there is danger that the delay is causing discouragement then it would be possible – though not otherwise necessary – to inaugurate, in the interim, "pilot" or "ice-breaker" ordinations of a very few *viri probati*. It would, however, be made clear that these do not constitute the final model which is the ordination of teams of community leaders.

The clergy will deliberate on the decisive influence the ordination of *viri probati* will have on their work and their life. The aspects of their traditional role that will be most affected are their public image, their future task among the many OCLs, and the celibacy which they themselves had to promise while it will not be required of the OCLs.

The priests will be concerned about their image and will ask: "who will I be if one day I will be surrounded by so many others who are also called 'priests' but who live a very different kind of life? Who will I be if the postmaster is à priest, the bus driver, the bank teller and so many others? Today everybody knows what a priest is, but what about tomorrow? A Catholic priest today has a clear and high image in the Church and in society. Must he not necessarily lose it if so many others are called 'priest' in future?"

The basic idea that the present priests will assume a new role once large numbers of OCLs are introduced is quite obvious. It is unlikely that priests really have to fear they would be confused with the OCLs. Most authors who are in favour of the ordination of local leaders have in some way suggested a new assisting and supervisory role for the theologically fully trained priests. [12] It is of course most important that this new role is thoroughly discussed with the present priests. They will themselves point out that in most areas the community leaders do not wish to assume a clerical image nor do their communities wish their ordained leaders to do

---

[12] Among others W. Burrows, New Ministries. The Global Context. ORBIS New York 1980. He suggests a role which could be that of a "dean" or "coordinator" or "mini bishop" (p. 128).

so. It will be pointed out that the very fact that not *one* leader but only a team is ordained will reduce the danger that they assume a clerical image. They will themselves not like to be called "Father" or "padre" and will not want to wear clerical dress. Where this tendency exists it will be important to counteract it in the earliest stages because it would endanger the overall vision of a community Church.

Many aspects of this new role of the existing priests will have to be discussed. The key question is of course the clear and convinced choice of option 3 as outlined above. This will include the division of tasks between the OCLs and the animator priests, the place where the animators live in the future and to what extent they work as a team, the way in which the bishop supports this new role and many other aspects. Discussions will also include the gradual way in which this is introduced. In some countries only few of the existing priests may initially be touched by this change of role while in others it will affect most of the priests right from the start.

This change in role may be experienced by some as painful: "I always felt I am a pastor, but when teams of OCLs appear, then I will no longer be pastor, shepherding the flock of a certain place because it will be the OCLs who give the sacraments, conduct the meetings, make the plans of the community. The role of pastor will actually fall away because they are part of that community. One could say that in future the community is pastoring itself through its own ordained leaders. That may be very good for them, but for me it means a disturbing change of role. To be a pastor was my life. Now, after many years of being a pastor it is deeply unsettling to abandon that role."

This kind of pain of updating their role will be experienced mainly by those who never parted with the role of being provider-priest. The others who had long ago changed their role of provider-pastor into that of an enabler-pastor of the local leaders will not feel that pain in this way. The difficulty will also be reduced through the fact that not all communities of a parish will immediately have their OCLs. In most dioceses a part of the parishes will continue for many years to rely for all priestly services on the full-time priest. He will change his role only gradually. A complete change of role is very many years away.

Discussions among the existing priests will also deal with the life style of the priests. The priests will point out that the new kind of priest, the ordained community leaders, are actually what were formerly called "secular priests." They truly belong to the secular sphere, the world of everyday life. They follow a secular profession and are married like everybody else. It is they now who are the "secular priests," not the present priests who do not live like others in the world, do not marry or take up secular work for a livelihood. The existing priests are more monastic than secular. When priests who live a truly secular way of life make an appearance, how will this affect the present diocesan priests who may be called "secular" but are in fact not secular? Will they not feel insecure? If their priesthood is of the same genre as that of the new secular diocesan priests, why should they not also marry?

The question must arise why the existing diocesan priests should remain non-secular and unmarried now that the Church accepts married *viri probati* priests. People and priests will want to know the fundamental reason for the very different mode of life of the existing priests. Many priests have adopted celibacy as a kind of condition without which they could not have been ordained. They have tried to establish a personal spiritual basis for their acceptance of celibacy but with the awareness that they only made a promise not to marry and did not vow celibacy as the members of religious institutes do. When they felt called to serve in the church they did not necessarily experience a vocation to celibacy but to priesthood. At the time there was only one access to priesthood and that required the candidates to promise celibacy. They were counseled that a celibate way of life was necessary to be totally available to God and the Church. Because of this obligatory condition they promised celibacy.

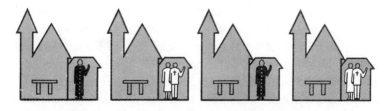

If we would make the mistake of introducing *viri probati* in such a way that in the future they would just work alongside married diocesan priests in the parishes, having no different role, then this promise which was somehow conditional must come under scrutiny. If one parish is served by a celibate priest, the next parish by a married *vir probatus* priest, the following one again by a celibate one, and so forth, then neither the people nor the priests will understand why there is a need that they follow different life styles. If there is hardly a difference in role, why should there be a difference in commitment?

The question will be felt most strongly by those celibate priests who have been continually struggling to remain celibate. They will be the first to raise the question: if celibate life is not the only way of becoming a priest, if it is no longer the indispensable condition, why must we existing priests remain celibate? The promise was freely made but at the time there was only the choice between becoming a celibate priest or remaining a layman. Now there is the added option of becoming a married part-time priest. Of course there will be speculations about a yet distant and hypothetical fourth possibility, a married full-time priest.

This way of thinking is pure logic and nobody will be able to silence the argument. Questions of this nature will be asked at a very early stage when the prevailing mood is one of wait-and-see. They will be more forcibly voiced once the number of ordained community leaders begins to increase, and increase they must.

Without a new role priests may lose their dedication

If priests are not helped during those early stages to discover their future new role, a gradual erosion of dedication and of priestly celibacy will be unavoidable. It was this very realistic fear which prompted a majority of the bishops at the world synod of 1971 to vote against the introduction of *viri probati* ordinations. Some, however, even today do not yet see this danger that the ordination of married proven Christians could cause a disintegration of the commitment of the present priests. They think it is sufficient to state that the discipline of the present priests is not altered when the ordination of *viri probati* is legislated. This may be possible legally, but humanly it is quite impossible.

To make ourselves more aware why it is humanly impossible to uphold the commitment of the present priests if they are not given a new role, we try to picture in the following hypothetical account what would probably happen in that case. We assume that in this case the Church authorities just announce a change of law, that the training of *viri probati* candidates just begins without further dialogue, that they are ordained and begin to function in the parishes which had no priest.

In areas where a larger number of ordained community leaders have thus begun working in the parishes but where the future way of life of the existing priests was not clarified, we can assume that after some time a substantial number of priests of those areas will ask to be allowed to marry while remaining in office. They want to marry in a proper way and will not just take their partner into the parish house or contract a civil marriage. Unlike many who left the priesthood over the past years, they wish to continue working as priests and to give good example. They are aware that the parish community will challenge an illegal partnership of a priest who remains in office.

The priests and their communities have themselves made the request for the introduction of OCLs in their parishes and we therefore presume that their communities have become accustomed to discuss all relevant matters openly with those priests. The OCLs will not advise the priests that they and their partners should just live openly in illegal unions but that they should seek official permission to marry. In this request for permission they will argue that the ordination of married men has created a new situation. They key element of the new situation is that they are fulfilling the same sacred functions and should therefore be allowed to freely choose to marry or to remain celibate.

When the bishops are approached they will at first react negatively but will eventually be impressed by the sheer logic of this argumentation and will urge Rome to grant such priests dispensation from their promise of celibacy and permit them to continue exercising their priestly office.

Still continuing our hypothetical forecast we have to assume that Rome would resist such a request, rightly fearing that the granting of dispensations in such circumstances will lead to the collapse of the law of celibacy. The initial refusal would, however, not end the matter. The demands for dispensation to marry will, in this new situation, appear too logical to be abandoned and will continue to be made until there is some sign of hope. A time of intensive negotiations would follow, during which many bishops concerned will point out that the situation is becoming ridiculous and untenable, that there is no possible explanation as to why the Church ordains married men for the priesthood while other diocesan priests had to leave priesthood if they got married. The bishops would also insist that the refusal to grant dispensations will lead to marriages which contravene canon law. Priests might just go ahead and solemnize their marriage claiming it is unjust to deny them the right. Public opinion in those areas would support the priests, making it virtually impossible for the bishop to suspend them and for Rome to remove the bishop who refuses to punish the breach of the law in these new circumstances.

Under such pressure dispensations will eventually be granted, probably only after a lengthy period of confusion and uncertainty. There may be instances where marriages of priests are celebrated in ways which appear legal but are not canonically correct. In other instances it might not be certain whether a married priest is continuing to officiate legally or not. Most likely only the pressure to redress increasingly illicit situations will eventually persuade Rome to grant dispensations which will be limited to certain areas or to individual dioceses.

A progressive disintegration of the traditional discipline of priests, such as the one described in this hypothetical account, would cause widespread unpleasantness and be a bad example to the members of the Church and to the world in general. Much of the idealism of the present priests would be compromised. Nothing can be gained from such unwonted proceedings but much will be lost. There must be another way of maintaining the well-proven traditional priesthood with its high ideals and sacrificial dimension. It is absolutely essential that the priests be guided towards a new vision of their place in the community and in the Church, and their new role as animators of the OCLs in the parish.

We need a religious community of diocesan priests

When *viri probati* priests are introduced in the manner of option 3, that is as teams of OCLs, they will be diocesan priests but will follow a way of life so different from the full-time diocesan priests that the dioceses now have two major kinds of diocesan priests. As we have seen above it is important that the existing diocesan priests become conscious of their distinct new role in their diocese as animators of the OCLs. If we were to make the mistake of emphasising nothing else than the fact that we now have an increased number of diocesan priests than before, then we would cause confusion. We would overlook or even downgrade the special vocation and the particular role of the full-time priests in the diocese.

The two kinds of priest have received distinct callings. The *viri probati* are called to combine secular life with priesthood and to serve the Church in their own community. The full-time priests are called to give their life totally in the service of not just one parish community but the whole diocese, in very close collaboration with the bishop. Their vocation differs in a similar manner as the vocation of Paul differed from that of the presbyters of Corinth, Ephesus, Thessalonia and the other communities of the early Church.

This important difference should be recognised in order to help the full-time priests to remain faithful to their vocation. In the past, priesthood meant only one clearly defined state. With the introduction of OCLs, the term must be qualified to distinguish between full-time and *viri probati* priests. There should be not only a theoretical distinction but, more importantly, also a practical one, a visible sign. One way of doing this is to create a religious community of diocesan priests.

We can assume that a good number of full-time priests have established in themselves a personal spiritual basis for their total dedication. Their spirit of self-giving is very similar to that of the members of religious institutes. Celibacy in the case of diocesan priests is by way of a promise, but for Religious it means a vow. The difference is in the definition but not in their dedication. The diocesan priests are just as resolved to devote their whole life to the service of others. Why not invite them to deepen the promises they already made by becoming more of a religious community around the bishop? By definition the presbyterium is already a community, but the new common task they will assume as animators could mold them into a brotherhood similar to the religious institutes. This would not mean joining an existing religious institute of a certain charism but establishing a religious community of diocesan priests.

There is no reason why such a religious community cannot be established in the diocese. At this point the details are not important and need not be spelled out here. Our interest lies in the effects a religious community would have at the time of dramatic change when a new kind of priest makes its appearance in the Church. Just as other religious communities have their special charism, the specific charism of the religious community of diocesan priests would be to build up the local Church together with the bishop.

We are proposing that simultaneously with the introduction of *viri probati* priests, the present priests are given their new role. They begin to participate more closely in the overseeing work of the bishop, become the animators and formators of the teams of ordained community leaders, be the link between the teams and the bishop and exercise their responsibilities living and working as teams. They are asked to give themselves totally to this new and decisive task just as they had been doing in their traditional role. They are invited to express this whole-hearted self-giving by becoming members of a religious community of diocesan priests.

The way in which the priests are introduced to the idea of their new role and invited to undertake it should be reassuring. The priests will accept it only if they see that the bishop himself is convinced of it and is also prepared to be the core of it. It should not constitute just a change in legislation but more so in relationship; the priests should understand that through it they will be drawn closer to the bishop and to each other. While legal pronouncements would have little effect, a meaningful appeal to the generosity of priests will be convincing.

Dioceses differ vastly from each other in extent, in the composition of their priests, and in their historical development. There are dioceses which comprise over a thousand diocesan priests plus priests of dozens of different religious institutes. There are small dioceses with as few as twenty priests; and in the Young Churches half of the priests in a small diocese belong to a religious institute, leaving only a handful of diocesan priests. Such a small number can of course not start a new religious community. However, they may already be a closely knit community around their bishop and this is what counts.

Reactions to the proposal to form a religious community of diocesan priests will differ from place to place. Some groups of priests may at first reject the idea and instead demand that celibacy should immediately become "optional," whatever meaning they give to that term. It will be important to realize that such a proposition would betray the goal of moving towards a community-based Church. The priests would then give priority to developing their personal life, to their marriage and to the establishment of a family home. They would naturally be very occupied with these concerns and have less time for building up the teams of OCLs. The establishment of these would be neglected and perhaps even postponed. We can develop the vision of a community Church only if we devote all our energy to the formation of teams of community leaders and the simultaneous formation of teams of animator priests. The future of those priests who feel that they cannot become members of animator-priest teams or join the new religious community of diocesan priests will have to be considered, but as a secondary concern. The order of precedence is crucial.

Dioceses who ask for the permission to ordain *viri probati* priests will therefore have to make sure that the introduction of the new priests and the future role of the existing priests are considered together and at the same time. Where reflection on the changed status of the latter group is neglected it is quite likely that the unintended process of a gradual erosion of priestly celibacy will follow.

Even where the concerns of both kinds of priest are considered together, reactions may differ considerably in the various dioceses. We can presume that there are dioceses where the majority of the priests will see the connection between the two issues, will be highly motivated towards making OCLs a success, and will therefore continue their self-giving as members of a new religious community of diocesan priests. It is necessary, however, also to foresee that there will be dioceses whose priests find it difficult to come to an agreement and may decide to postpone the whole process. Again other dioceses may not even begin dialogue sessions because there are indications that no agreement will be reached.

In some dioceses the priests will not like the idea of a religious community of diocesan priests although they nevertheless clearly indicate that the majority of them will continue to serve as they always did. They may find it unfair to expect them to modify their commitment officially at the very time when things are unclear and are changing. They are aware that they will be required to work next to married priests, but they have worked next to married leaders for a long time. They will not be confused by the introduction of this new kind of priests. Though no immediate formal establishment of a religious community of diocesan priests takes place, the bishop is assured of having a core group of dedicated co-workers during the time of change. Without any official inauguration, there exists in fact a communal dedication that serves the same purpose. The formal establishment is still desirable but can follow later. The very fact that the relevant issues are discussed publicly will be helpful and will enable the priests and their bishop to go ahead with the introduction of teams of ordained community leaders. Group reflections of this kind will ensure that there is no need to fear any kind of disintegration after local teams are ordained.

One may feel tempted to call this core group of priests close to the bishop the "presbyterium." In a later chapter, "Forming one presbyterium to include several kinds of priest," we will see that it is better this term remains as it is and that also in future it includes all different kinds of priest, including the animator priests and the OCLs.

If the above considerations are correct, it would mean that there is a way to introduce *viri probati* without endangering the commitment of the existing priests, a most important factor because it makes it possible for bishops' conferences to agree on introducing *viri probati* in some of their dioceses although other dioceses find it impossible to do so at the time.

We can introduce the new kind of priests without losing the existing priests

Is it possible or not to introduce *viri probati* without endangering the dedication of the diocesan priests? This crucial question has been answered in different ways. [13] The question is asked because married men officiating as priests will make it appear as though celibacy is now optional for all diocesan priests. The sudden introduction of *viri probati* before the present priests are fully prepared to accept the change could be a shock and cause them great uncertainty, de-motivate many and gravely affect the laity. It could lead to an avalanche of problematic changes.

It is difficult to foretell the future but it is important to attempt a forecast because it is this aspect concerning the introduction of *viri probati* that would be the greatest obstacle to the bishops of the world arriving at a decision. The bishops would be divided on the issue. The majority would find it too difficult to cope with the avalanche of changes which would follow if at the same time *viri probati* are introduced or very soon afterwards a change would have to be made to the law of priestly celibacy. They would insist that the present ministry structure of having only one kind of priest must not be endangered. Only a smaller number of bishops would prefer to face the probable changes than to continue with the present situation of priest shortage and would feel confident that they could handle them. It would be practically impossible for the bishops of the world to come to a consensus at this time.

The same problem would arise within the individual bishops' conferences. If the decision were left to particular conferences, there would again be many bishops who would refuse to allow the introduction of *viri probati* anywhere if they have reason to fear this would cause tensions and defections everywhere. It is therefore necessary to think ahead how the introduction of OCLs will affect the existing priests.

In doing so, we should keep three stages in mind. These are depicted in the diagram which shows combined parishes which symbolically are shown as clusters of five parishes served by one priest. This is just a

---

[13]   The 25 bishops who in 1970 asked for *viri probati* priests (see footnote 1) said they wanted (and presumably thought they would be able) to retain the present law of priestly celibacy; R. Hickey, op.cit, is of the same opinion. In private many hold the opposite view. The writer has also, in earlier versions of this study paper, expressed the opposite opinion and is now changing his stance. What made him change his view was the realization that a consistent emphasis of the new role of animator priests will make it possible to maintain the commitment of the present priests.

symbolic figure because in reality some cluster-parishes actually consist of only two or three parishes in the Older Churches, and of ten to twenty Church communities in the Young Churches. The clusters of five Churches are intended to symbolise the average situation where a shortage of priests has arisen, where one priest has to serve several parishes and where therefore the altar often remains empty.

The stage of priest shortage: Many altars remain empty. There is only one kind of priest,  overburdened, frustrated, but feeling secure.

Transition stage: —

A few parishes have introduced OCLs. The re-  maining priests see the new vision, prepare for it, continuing faithfully in their work.

Post-transition stage: Many parishes now have OCLs and try to make  the new vision a success. Among the other parishes some priests try but feel unable, others dislike it. All continue in their task.

The key idea during the transition-stage, as explained in the previous chapter, is to dialogue with the existing priests and with all concerned on the new vision of Church. In this way the priests, the leaders, and the communities become aware that we are not only introducing one new kind of priest but are at the same time developing the new role of the animator priest. Two new kinds of priest are introduced, not only one.

Diocesan priests are people with ideals. They will realize that they are invited to contribute to a historic development, influencing not only their own lives but the lives of all members of the Church. For this great task they are asked to spend all their time and exercise all their idealism as they have done in the past for the traditional model of Church. Their new role may even revitalize the idealism of some priests.

The middle section of the above diagram shows the transition stage and draws attention to the changing scene, the dawning of a new way of life in the parish. Only a small percentage of priests (one in five in the example of our diagram) have become animator priests. The majority continue to reflect on whether they and their parishes are ready to take this decisive step. Of these, some are partially prepared, others await the progress of events. If the transition stage is introduced and carried through in a vision-orientated way, we can assume that the great majority of priests will remain dedicated to their vocation.

Let us now turn to the post-transition stage, because many may agree that during the initial phase the dedication of the existing priests can be

upheld but may have doubts how the ideal of total dedication of priests can be continued at a later stage. We now think about a time which lies perhaps one generation after OCLs have become numerous in the dioceses and have even become a normal feature of the diocese.

The diagram illustrates the stage when more and more communities have OCLs. In one after the other of the communities people gradually accept the idea of community-oriented Church and of the ordination of their leaders. Only in a minority of communities we see that the altar still remains empty on many Sundays.

After many years of having OCLs officiate in the parish everybody is used to the two kinds of priest, the ordained community leaders and the animator priests. The full-time priests of the post-transition stage have not experienced the emotions of the earlier stage of transition. They received their vocation when this diversity of ministry was already taken for granted. The diagram shows realism in presupposing that a number of parishes will remain without OCLs and the traditional kind of priest will continue to administer all sacraments in those communities. Though a majority of parishes and of priests will have accepted teams of OCLs, the changed ministry structure will not have reached all the parishes and all the priests.

The question now is: during the post-transition period, will the Church accept for full-time priesthood candidates who are married or who intend to marry? The most likely reply will be negative.

Let us take a practical example. A young man goes to the bishop and asks to become a married priest. He is asked what he means by being a priest. If he replies by describing the traditional priest who all by himself cares for the people he is given to understand that this kind of provider-priest will not exist in the long term future of the diocese. If his description fits to the animator priest he is advised that this important task needs the giving of one's whole life and he is invited to join the religious community of diocesan priests. If, however, his idea of priesthood resembles that of the *viri probati* whom he sees every day in his community, he is told to work first for his community in many other ways until his community asks him to accept more and more responsibility and finally approaches him with the request to become one of their ordained community leaders. He is given these two options, but not the option of becoming a full-time married priest. Even if the Church law were one day to allow this, the diocese would be very careful to choose only those with the qualities to become the "spiritual motor" which the animator priest must be in future.

If the same young man goes to a particular community and asks to become a priest, members of the community will ask him the same questions and he will get similar replies. In other words: the phrase "optional celibacy" so common today will not even be mentioned. Most probably it will have been forgotten by that time.

We have also to consider possible requests from more adult persons in the post-transition stage. How will the bishop respond to a married ordained local leader who asks to become a full-time animator priest and all the circumstances indicate that this is for the good of the Church? The response will have to be positive.

What if on the side of the animator priests, one of them were to ask the bishop for permission to marry as he feels he can no longer continue in the priesthood as a celibate, and again all the circumstances indicate that this is for the good of the Church? Such permissions will be refused at the beginning of the post-transition period but later they will be granted.

In the earlier stage, the good of the Universal Church will take precedence and the priest will be advised rather to request laicization. The decision may appear harsh but is necessary at the time to prevent a distortion of the basic vision. The marriage of the existing priests should not mistakenly be seen as the aim. The creation of a community Church through OCLs must stand out as the main focus. The personal difficulty of the one or the other of the existing priests is understandable but should not detract from the actual aim during the initial stage. At a later stage when the overall thrust has become clear, there will be less need for stressing this priority. By that time all are well used to the parallel existence of the two kinds of priest. If by that time an exceptional celibate priest pleads for getting married while continuing to work as a priest and all indications are that he will continue to make an important contribution to the life of the Church as a married priest, then it is most likely that the general opinion will be that permission should be granted. Instances of the above nature will, however, be the exception; the common pattern will be thousands of married OCLs and a small number of fully dedicated animator priests. The number of exceptions a diocese will grant in the post-transition stage will be influenced by the local situation. It will depend primarily on the image of the presbyterate which the diocese wants to create and to some extent also on the financial means of the diocese.

The main thesis of this chapter is that we can introduce the new kind of priest without losing the existing priests. This will, however, only be possible if the dioceses present a new vision to their priests and their communities, and will be impossible if they merely issue a new decree.

Insisting on authority and issuing decrees will certainly not be sufficient in the many conflict situations which will arise, such as the one we have just mentioned. It will be difficult for the bishop to remove from office those few priests who during the time of transition break ranks with the majority of priests and get married while insisting on continuing to work as priests. The difficulty will be that such priests may get much public backing for their demand to remain in office while getting married. The media and large parts of the public will find it easy to put pressure on the bishop to leave the priest in office. They will find it easy to point out that it would be a contradiction to remove one priest from ministry because of his marriage and at the same time to invite many married men to enter the same ministry.

The bishop could well find himself in a dilemma in such cases. If he remains firm and removes the priest, his valuable project may be given a bad image to the extent that cooperation becomes difficult. If on the other hand he gives in and allows the priest to continue in office while getting married the project becomes endangered from the other side. The neighbouring dioceses and the universal Church will accuse him of disloyalty, of endangering their own project, and of transgressing canon law. His own priests would also become divided. Many of them will feel betrayed, will refuse to cooperate in the project and will insist it should be abandoned while others will now see a reason to renounce their earlier promise of loyal cooperation and will rather insist on the abolition of the law of celibacy.

Even if it is only a small number of priests who would break away from their earlier promise of loyal cooperation and would now insist on getting married while remaining in office, the whole project could be endangered in this way.

The best preparation for this kind of problem is to ensure that the whole undertaking is started only after a very solid and wide backing is established. A wide backing means several things. It means that the whole body of priests has discussed the matter openly and repeatedly, has been made aware of the need for a united approach, and has given a clear undertaking to support it. It means that many dialog sessions have been held in the parishes. It further means that the diocesan pastoral council has several times considered the feasibility of the project and that other laity groupings and larger assemblies of the laity have decided to support the project. A diocesan synod can finally sum up and officially declare to follow this route. If so much backing by priests and laity is assured it will be quite unlikely that the publicity campaign of a few limited cases could become disruptive.

If it is only the bishop who becomes the target of some local campaign it will be difficult for him to defend the project because it is in itself an idealistic one. Ideals are always easy to attack and difficult to defend in public controversies. If, however, it will not be the bishop but a fairly representative body which replies to disruptive campaigns of this kind, the chances of maintaining the ideal in public are much higher.

All this re-enforces our earlier insistence that the whole process should be preceded by public dialog on the widest basis. We have already seen several reasons for this public and open approach and realize now that even the later development of this process emphasizes this methodology.

The successful introduction of teams of OCLs without losing the dedication of the present priests will also be assisted by completely avoiding the phrase "optional celibacy." The use of the phrase will increase the problems because it presupposes a process which we will definitely not choose and which is totally different from what is suggested here. It points to a possible sudden change of Church law which would give the present priests a choice whether or not to continue with the promise they made to remain celibate, and give the option to candidates for the priesthood to marry or not. The phrase is therefore totally unsuitable for describing the process outlined here. It would mislead the debate and should therefore not be used in discussions pertaining to the introduction of two new kinds of priest.

At the completion of this chapter, we reiterate that the reaction of the present priests as described in the above pages is based on the assumption that it is option 3 of *viri probati* which is being implemented, teams of OCLs. It is only with this option in mind that one can invite the existing priests to assume a new role and dedicate their whole life to accomplishing it. If dioceses were to choose an "easier" option then they could not speak of a new role for the existing priests and would have little reason to appeal to them to continue in their complete self-dedication. In many areas of the Church an attractive "easier" option could be something like option 2 where one would ordain not teams of OCLs but only one good proven person here and there in order to alleviate the scarcity of sacraments. That would mean having an additional provider-priest next to the present one. Both would fulfill the same role of pastor and spiritual animator, the difference being only that one works full time and the other part time. As we have seen above, that would make it impossible to answer the question why one should observe the evangelical counsel of celibacy and the other not.[14] This consideration reminds us again how important it is to choose carefully the most suitable option among the possible kinds of *viri probati* priests.

---

[14] A good number of Anglican dioceses have followed this option of ordaining iso-

The new role among the many other roles

When we speak of a new role for the full-time priests we certainly do not mean that this would be the *only* role exercised by the ministerial priesthood of the Church. The same must be born in mind when we emphasise that we need two new kinds of priest, the teams of OCLs and the animator priests. We certainly do not mean that these should be the only kinds of priests in the Church. The two new kinds of priests must be emphasised because in our view their combined existence is the precondition for a sound introduction of the ordination of *viri probati*.

It is obvious that the many other roles exercised by priests today should continue unhindered. We need priests who serve the Church as administrators, others as leaders and members of religious institutes, others as scientists and theologians.

The only model of priesthood which will have to recede gradually is the one of the provider priest. This is the logical consequence of introducing the two new kinds of the OCLs and their animators. Even this reduction of the provider priest will not be an enforced one or a sudden one but will proceed in gradual stages, though in a clearly intentional way.

Even when we consider the new role of the animator priests, we should not imagine that their only and exclusive task is the formation, training and coordination of the OCLs. This new role has to be emphasized in order to make the introduction of the OCLs possible, but there is no need to exercise it in an exclusive way. It can be combined with many roles as far as the situation allows this.

In several publications we were reminded that people of sophisticated societies need the highly qualified pastor who attends to their complicated spiritual needs, and we should therefore not envisage having no other kind of priest than the enabler-priests who move from community to community and have little chance to attend to the spiritual needs of individuals. There

---

lated part-time "auxiliary priests" and seem to be satisfied with this solution. However, since their full-time clergy was already married, it is obvious that this step did not question the life-style of the existing clergy. That example can therefore not serve as model for Catholic dioceses.

can be specialist priests next to them, but it may also be possible that some priests combine several roles.

The role of spiritual guide can be combined with the role of being animator and enabler of other priests. Two roles of this kind could be combined in several ways. One way is that the majority of the full-time priests work as animation teams of a large number of parishes with OCLs and are completely occupied only with this animation work, while a minority of the full-time priests work in spiritual centres. Those in need of deeper spiritual counseling go to those centres of their area. Another way is to make the cluster-parishes a bit smaller so that the animator priests can at the same time offer spiritual weekends, spiritual courses, counseling hours. A combination of these patterns is also possible.

If the dioceses have a large number of OCLs there will be an increased need for several kind of specialised centres in between the parishes. Some will be centres of formation, others for theology, others for spirituality and counseling. It will become more necessary to have a diversity of such centres and it will also be easier because the priests with full theological training are no longer over-burdened with providing the day-to-day pastoral care in the parishes on their own. The presence of many OCLs will make it easier for full-time priests to fulfill specialised roles.

How to prepare for the ordination of community leaders.

A list of preconditions before dioceses can introduce *viri probati*

As already stressed, dioceses which intend introducing the ordination of community leaders must give the assurance to other dioceses and to other groups that they will do so in accordance with sound principles.

This is necessary so as to win the consent of others and to avoid developments from going wrong.

One way of reassuring others is to allow only those to introduce OCLs who fulfill a list of preconditions which should be very practical if they are to be effective. A mere exhortation or vague statement could be damaging to the proceedings and would not be trusted by neighbouring dioceses. It is up to the dioceses and the bishops' conference to draw up their own lists. The following list is an indication of the kind of questions that need to be answered affirmatively.

Before a diocese begins the ordination of teams of community leaders it should be able to give replies in the affirmative to all the following questions:

a)   Have the great majority of the priests studied the various types of *viri probati*? Are they convinced that only the ordination of **teams** of community leaders (OCLs) should be undertaken? Have they reacted positively to the "List of preconditions for parishes"?

b)   Have almost all the priests of the diocese participated in a prolonged process of considering the effects which the OCLs will have on their own ministry?

c)   Have the priests accepted the idea of an intensified form of presbyterium or of a religious community of diocesan priests? If not, have they indicated in a reliable way that they will continue to serve the church with the same dedication even after OCLs are introduced?

d)   Have the necessary arrangements been made to begin immediately to enable priests to lead the communities to the stage where OCLs can be introduced, and to prepare them for their own new future role as formators and animators?

e)   Have practical plans been formulated to move gradually towards the establishment of teams of priests, teams who will fulfill the role of formators and animators of OCLs?

Of course, dioceses are independent and cannot be forced to comply with the preconditions drawn up by others or by their conference. It is, however, possible that they themselves volunteer to adopt the same list in order to come to a common decision of the whole conference. They will find it easier to convince their neighbouring dioceses and the whole bish-ops' conference that this methodology is safe if they can demonstrate that they have taken all precautions. The need to convince neighbouring dioceses is apparent from the precedent of the permanent diaconate. When the permanent diaconate was instituted, individual dioceses were not permitted to introduce it on their own. Their bishops' conference had to decide in principle that within the territory of the conference the individual dioceses could begin.

There are indeed several reasons why dioceses should use dialog sessions and lists of preconditions in order to ensure broad backing for this huge innovation of introducing the ordination of teams of community leaders. There may nevertheless be dioceses which find this open approach impossible. They should be aware that alternatives which seem to be easier and quicker may eventually run into serious difficulties such as a public outcry why celibacy is not abolished altogether for diocesan priests. If a diocese is unable to undertake the process through widespread backing by all sides, it should rather wait until majority backing can be assured. Dioceses which do begin the process through dialog but during this process realize that either the priests or the laity are too divided should postpone the project to a later time.

Some will say it is impossible to begin the process of dialogue and then abort it. It is of course true that many would be deeply disappointed if a development which seemed to them to be a historic chance would be postponed. Experience has, however, shown that the forward-looking group is usually more cooperative and more prepared to compromise than the tradition-oriented group. It is therefore more likely that a postponement will lead to a long process of reflections, discussions, methods of community building, experimental forms of sharing of ministries and other developments which are favourable for an eventual consensus. A postponement therefore seems to offer more hope than a militant approach of forcing the project to go ahead against large opposition.

A list of preconditions before parishes can apply for the ordination of their community leaders

After the bishops' conference has given the green light and after the diocese has made its decision, not all parishes should automatically be entitled to ask for the ordination of some of their community leaders. Certain criteria must be established, not only for the individual candidates but also for the parish as a whole. A list of preconditions for parishes should be drawn up and well publicised throughout the entire diocese. It will form the basis for the many discussions we can expect in the parishes and serve as an indication of the way the parishes should develop. It will also prevent parishes which are conscious of nothing else than of the dire need of priests from rushing to the bishop with the dangerous plea to ordain immediately one outstanding individual person.

The following questionnaire exemplifies the standard of readiness required by a parish:

Before a parish can apply for the ordination of a team of its community leaders it should be able to give a positive reply to the following questions:

a) Can the priest(s) of this parish accompany ordained community leaders (OCLs)?

b) Has the parish had a team of deacons for at least two years who in future could form a team of OCLs? Has the team proved over this period that it can conduct liturgical services in rotation and together with other leaders of the parish? Is the team well accepted by the parish? Has it played a commendable leadership role in the parish council and in the parish as a whole?

c) Is the parish accustomed to a general sharing of work, and to having several leaders for the various tasks? Is the parish ready to cooperate with those who fulfill these offices? Do the parishioners support the idea of voluntary service, with no remuneration for work done? Does the parish prefer teamwork to individuals undertaking tasks? Does it favour the rotation of office bearers? Does it show good participation in the election of candidates for all ministries?

d) Is the parish accustomed to reflect together on the path the parish should follow? Is shared decision-making an accepted practice?

e) Has the parish succeeded in developing some critical spirit or does it follow any leader blindly even if s/he violates the way of the gospel seriously? Is the parish able to find ways of correcting mistakes made by leaders, especially those which affect the whole parish?

f) Does the parish and do its leaders accept the idea of ongoing formation?

Each diocese, bishops' conference, or the whole country can devise its own list of preconditions. The list should not omit clauses which stress the importance of teamwork and of voluntary service. It can contain additional conditions such as the establishment of Small Christian Communities, Justice-and-Peace committees and other community-centred organizations.

A publicized list of preconditions will make it clear from the start that the scarcity of the sacraments is not a sufficient reason for allowing a particular parish to introduce OCLs. We must foresee possible instances where the main thrust of parishes in asking for OCLs is the alarmingly low frequency of availability of the sacraments. We reiterate that this policy could lead to problems much more difficult to rectify than the scarcity of the sacraments.

In many dioceses the majority of parishes is not yet ready to introduce OCLs. These parishes must be given the reasons as to what is lacking and be properly informed about how to prepare themselves to introduce OCLs. The dioceses should therefore be very careful in drawing up a list of preconditions.

It will be advisable for the bishop or a team delegated by him to visit a parish which asks for permission to introduce OCLs. It would be too risky to give this permission without knowing the parish well.

In numerous discussions with people who were eager that the Church should allow the introduction of *viri probati* we could hear people concentrating on only one point: "we are certain we have a suitable candidate in our parish." Even many publications use the same phrase and give the impression that they know of only one precondition: that there must be a suitable candidate. Realizing that so many view the question from a narrow perspective it will be important to emphasize a list of preconditions.

Preparation through dialogue meetings

In an earlier chapter we discussed the need to conduct dialogue sessions on the global idea of ordaining *viri probati* and to initiate dialogue sessions in the dioceses, the purpose of which is to disseminate general awareness and information. We now consider a different kind of dialogue sessions, in parishes which have reached a much more advanced stage, the stage where they have to make the final decision whether or not to ask for the ordination of some of the leaders of their own particular parish.

We must presume that in those cases the general permission for selected parishes to have community leaders ordained has already been granted. For some time the parishes have been acquainted with the list of preconditions they have to fulfill. Several parishes have been putting these conditions into practice and have reached the stage demanded. They have undergone a long process of community building and sharing of ministries and are ready to apply to the bishop for the ordination of some of their leaders. Each parish has now to make its own immediate preparations for the inception of OCLs.

This final phase should again include several dialogue meetings to arrive at a consensus of the community that this parish ask the bishop for the permission to have a team of OCLs.

As in the case of the diocesan meetings, these too should be conducted by a mixed team of priests and lay leaders, consist not of lectures but of free exchange of opinions, include discussion in smaller groups so that all have a chance to speak their mind and pose their questions. Great care should be taken that opposing views can be voiced freely.

The whole congregation should become aware of the many issues involved: how candidates will eventually be chosen, where they will be trained, what feelings might arise against them, how they should receive encouragement from the community, how the community could criticize them, why they should function as a team and not as individuals, what authority they will have, what position they will hold in the parish council, how they should be addressed, why they would not be expected to wear clerical dress, how they will work together with all the other leaders and helpers in the community, why their ordination will not cause the other leaders to become redundant, how the priests will work with them and what they will do for them, and other similar concerns.

When the differences among the three main options were discussed in Part One, it became clear that option 3 actually completes and implements the vision of Vatican II, the art of doing things together. Dialogue sessions are therefore integral to this vision of Church and to the way OCLs should come into being and function in the future. They would definitely not be monopolistic but would fit into the overall network of an active community.

The opportunity to dialogue will reduce the anger of those less happy about introducing OCLs. They at least have a chance to voice their feelings and will be less tempted to see a schism as the only possible reaction. Dialogue will also make it clear that adjustments to the sharing of ministry will always be possible and can be considered jointly by the whole community.

The need for dialogue sessions at all stages, including the final stages when the decision seems already clear, is evident when we keep in mind that difficulties will almost certainly arise during the implementation. We described one of those possible difficulties earlier when we mentioned the possibility that some priests may step out of line and the media whip up opposition at the bishops for not immediately abolishing celibacy in its totality. Controversies and clashes of this kind can be faced in a much more convincing way if dialogue sessions have produced a broad consensus. Without broad consensus it will appear as if only the narrow-mindedness of the pope and the bishops was the reason for choosing the high road of building up teams of OCLs instead of simply abolishing celibacy.

The number of dialog sessions will vary from place to place. In some countries and parishes, particularly in Young Churches, the parishes have already gone through a long process of community building. Their normal *modus operandi* is that of self-ministering communities. When they will one day reach the stage of deciding on introducing OCLs, they will obviously need fewer dialogue sessions in order to reach consensus on this question.

In other areas, especially in the Older Churches, a much greater number of dialogue meetings will be needed in order to move away from the idea of being cared for by the clergy. Dialogue sessions will thus be adapted to the local situation.

Preparation through "group-conducted liturgies"

A very practical and sound preparation of the community would be the early introduction of a team-oriented way of celebrating Holy Mass and of conducting baptisms and funerals, long before the ordination of OCLs.

In "group-conducted liturgies" of this kind the priest no longer conducts the ceremony alone, but always together with two or more local leaders who wear liturgical garb. During the Eucharist the priest delegates as many parts of the rite as possible to the leaders next to him.

The main motive for group-conducted liturgies is the need to avoid tensions, splits and disunity in the parish when OCLs are introduced. The shock will be greatly reduced in this way. By the time a married member of the local community celebrates Holy Mass, the faithful are already used to seeing several such candidates standing next to the priest and slowly taking over the less essential parts of the celebration. The threatening thought of "Will the day really dawn when Mr. N will replace Father at the altar?" will gradually wear away. Other anxious questions will eventually be eroded if long before the ordination of community leaders, even before the ordination of deacons, the faithful see not only Mr. N on Sunday after Sunday but others as well in liturgical dress at the altar. Moreover, on some Sundays, the people will see Mr. N not among the liturgical team at the altar but as one of themselves, as part of the congregation in the nave of the Church. The candidates who are living like everyone else among their neighbours for the whole week will feel less exposed in this way, and the community can slowly change its expectations.

Group-conducted liturgies will also reduce the anxiety about the exclusion or inclusion of women in liturgical teams. Women are often already part of liturgical teams and to exclude them at the time when the question of ordination arises could be very painful. It is in any case clear that not all the members of liturgical teams will be ordained and that not all of them are permitted to fulfill the same function. If the congregation becomes used to the fact that all liturgies are conducted by teams of different kinds of leaders then this variety of team members can continue even when one day a few of them will have been ordained and others not.

Preparation of the animator priests and other animators

Well before a parish can ask for the introduction of OCLs, its fulltime priests must prove their ability to accompany the OCLs. There are indications that at least two-thirds of the present priests have the potential to do so. They must be trained and equipped with skills and materials for exercising this role.

The preparatory steps for equipping the priests for this task should be undertaken at the level of the diocese, with some assistance on the level of the bishops' conference. Several years may be needed in some dioceses for the adaptation of the priests, though this depends very much on the previous experience of the priests of the diocese in this kind of process. Priests who are unable to accompany OCLs will not work in parishes where they are introduced.

The key requirement is attitude: the wish to accompany leaders who bear full responsibility. The word "accompany" is one which has spontaneously arisen among those priests who are already fulfilling this role for their well-trained lay leaders. They realized that this term indicates quite well that in this role one does something different from directing, controlling, administering. The term "supervision" does not apply in its colloquial meaning of control, but applies very well in its technical sense of advice, dialogue, counsel, assistance. The term "accompanying" also indicates that one is always present in some way of brotherly assistance. The priests who accompany co-responsible leaders want to indicate that they try to be always interested, always keen on listening to the joys and difficulties, always available to assist. They do not abandon those who accept real responsibility. The term also indicates that everybody is aware that we are on a journey. We know very well that we are still far from what we want to be. We know very well of the shortcomings but are willing to press ahead together.

Attitudes of this kind can grow in most priests, because most of them possess a seed of these attitudes already. Attitudes are caught, not taught. Priests take part in events, in meetings, in training sessions and evaluate afterwards. This helps them to adjust their attitudes. One does not get a certificate for attitudes, but one gradually moves along towards such attitudes. A diocese which wants to foster these attitudes will ensure that there is ample opportunity to take part in events of this kind.

There are also skills required of animator priests, of religious who work as pastoral animators and of other pastoral workers. The most important skill for accompanying OCLs will be to conduct attractive meetings and training sessions with them. It is not so much the increased knowledge which is needed but the manner of conducting the meetings. They must be inviting, friendly, considerate and encouraging. OCLs will learn when they are happy, have courage, have confidence, are open with each other. OCLs are voluntary workers which means their formation sessions will mainly take place after work or on weekends. There would be plenty of reasons to excuse themselves from the meetings. They will take part under great sacrifices if they find the meetings enjoyable and useful.

Part of this skill of conducting enjoyable formation sessions is the ability to find ways of learning things in an easy and clear way. Lecture methods are least suitable for adults who learn in their spare time. Group work, visual aids, self-discovery methods are the favoured methods for adult learning. The diocese will offer many workshops to the future animators in order to familiarise all of them with these methods. In many areas much of this methodology is already known.

There is as yet no minimum curriculum for theological, scriptural and pastoral items to be learnt by OCLs but it will not be difficult to establish it. Neither will it be too difficult to familiarise the priest animators with the ways in which they can help the OCLs to acquire the necessary knowledge.

Preparation of the candidates

The target vision must be that OCLs emerge from active parish communities, remain integrated into them and work as teams within their communities. If they emerge in this way from the daily life of active parishes they will not develop into monopolisers but will continue to reflect together with the whole community after their ordination, work closely with the many other leaders and decide together with them.

To attain this vision it will be important to avoid all forms of status seeking from the beginning. This means that the parish should never ask for volunteers for becoming OCLs. The long journey of training must start with nothing else in the mind than working for the community and certainly not with the motive of becoming ordained. Only when the trainees have been working and training in this general way for many years could the question of ordination to the permanent diaconate be posed carefully. Dioceses with a long experience of the permanent diaconate have found that training should begin only in this manner and never with the express aim of the diaconate. Status seeking is extremely prevalent and this is one efficacious way of preventing it.

Beginning the training without aiming at a particular office is also important for another reason: it avoids a time scale. If a certain ordination requires a fixed number of years as the period of preparation, then a kind of "right to be ordained" exists. This is normal for residential seminaries but is most unsuitable for emergent leaders and also for OCLs. In parish situations the setting of a time table tends to put the emphasis on academic criteria, and tempts candidates to ask for ordination for the sole reason of not being "left behind." When speaking about the length of training, we should never give a definite number of years but only offer estimates and include more than one estimate. If there is no time schedule, candidates will become used to the principle of their training being open-ended, to be carried on after their ordination and to continue as ongoing formation.

Ongoing, unending formation is not limited to the OCLs. It must be universal practice for all forms of ministry including the non-ordained, in order to avoid any danger that formation might gradually stop after some time. If only the ordained have to continue with formation it would certainly be in danger of disappearing. The experience of other Churches has shown how easy it is to gradually neglect such formation, reduce it again and again, and eventually to drop it altogether. It must therefore be part of the preparation work to introduce ongoing formation for all kinds of ministry, not only for the OCLs.

Possible stages of formation and training

Dioceses which already have a healthy and effectively functioning permanent diaconate consisting of teams who emerged from among the communities will be able to complete the process in two years or even less.

Dioceses which do not yet have deacons but have similar teams of very well accepted, community-related and adequately trained lay leaders should not despise the stage of the permanent diaconate. Even if the ministry of the permanent deacon is not clearly defined and does not consist of clearly defined new tasks, it is nevertheless an important learning stage for all sides, for the animators, for the communities, and for the candidates. It must not be overlooked that the selection of the candidates for the permanent diaconate involves all sides in a much more serious way than the selection of lay leaders who could withdraw at any time. The permanent diaconate presents a definite commitment for life which is a new challenge to the lay leaders and to all others. Experience has shown that all sides realize afterwards that they had much to learn through this phase of the permanent diaconate. It would be a mistake to say that diaconate is not needed and that all those processes will be learnt when the candidates for OCLs are selected. Dioceses which are at the stage of having well trained lay leaders but not yet deacons may take something like five years until the ordination of OCLs. Such dioceses should begin the whole process with a series of dialogue sessions which alone may take about six months.

The diaconate will probably have to undergo some changes if OCLs are introduced. Otherwise the diaconate would again disappear as a ministry of its own and would again become a mere stepping stone to priesthood. At the same time the diaconate should then be designed in such a way that it will form a meaningful component in communities which have teams of ordained leaders. Suggestions for the adaptation of the diaconate to these new situations will need more room and must be presented on other occasions.

Dioceses which have lay leaders but have not placed much emphasis on unending ongoing formation of all leaders and on ways of community building will have to foresee a much longer process. They have to begin with awareness sessions of a different kind. They should not begin by immediately talking about the ordination of local leaders. They must first become aware of the need to be a community, of the need to let many charisms emerge from among the community, and of the need for an attitude of service. If the potential leaders aim at a high office from the start, their motivation gets confused. The first motivation must simply be to follow the gospel and to serve the community and the people, without any desire to reach certain offices or ranks.

Without even talking about ordinations of any kind the parish consolidates the formation of a great variety of teams of lay leaders for all kinds of ministries. This alone may take up to two years or longer. The parish

introduces an annual evaluation of all leaders, an annual training season
or a method of continuous training, and an annual liturgy of re-dedication
and blessing of all leaders.

After several years, another round of dialogue meetings precedes the
selection of candidates for the permanent diaconate. In several places the
training of deacons has taken three, five or more years. Two years or so
after the ordination of the deacons, a further dialogue session takes place
to select the candidates to be ordained for the priesthood. Then their final
training can start. Two or more years later they could be ordained as OCLs.

Besides considering the long time spans needed it will also be important to consider the tasks which will arise on various levels.

Several tasks will arise for the diocesan structures: Training
programmes have to be drawn up for the various situations and several
questions will arise. It has to be clarified whether there is a need for
stipulating varying lengths of preparation time for the different situations
within the diocese, avoiding however any definite time scale. It has to be
considered whether an individual diocese can afford to have different training courses within its territory.

Other questions will have to be clarified on the level of the bishops'
conference. Will training standards be uniform in all territories of a bishops' conference or can they differ according to the various situations? Is
there a need to determine minimum standards for certain areas?

How to sustain a structure of ordained
community leaders

The presence of a few exceptional OCLs will not cause any real problem in the initial stage. However, as we saw above, it is likely that in
many places the number will soon increase and this will pose a challenge
of how to sustain the new structure in the Church. The question how the
parish will in future maintain the quality of its OCLs should already be

discussed during the time leading up to the final decision about introducing OCLs.

It is first necessary to visualize what this challenge will mean for the full-time priests and bishops before offering concrete suggestions for maintaining unity and order in the structure.

Linking the teams of ordained community leaders with the animator priests

In the present situation it is clear to every priest that he has to visit every one of the many scattered communities he serves. He carefully makes a plan which ensures that no community, however distant it may be, remains for a long time without a visit from him. What convinces him of this need is the principle that no community should be without the sacraments for too long. He has other reasons as well for paying these regular visits to all his communities: planning for future events; training of leaders, the occasional need to settle difficulties that have arisen, and other Church business. It is however mainly the first motive of providing the sacraments, which moves even the less-committed to undertake visits despite the effort and the difficulties involved.

This situation will change if most communities have their own small team of ordained community leaders. Priests will no longer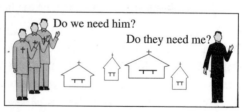
say "I must go to visit because they have not received the sacraments for so long...." The communities now have recourse to the sacraments through the OCLs. Will the animator priests continue their regular visits because of other motives? Will they feel responsible for animating and training the leaders? Will not a good number of animator priests even feel reluctant to make visits because they doubt whether they have something to offer which the OCLs cannot give? Will not a number of animator priests feel unable to influence the OCLs and the communities and therefore find excuses for staying away?

The very talented ones among the present priests will not find it difficult to ensure that the communities are eager to receive their visit. But what about the less talented ones?

Quite a few dioceses of Young Churches are already speaking of "absentee priests" who easily find excuses for being anywhere but in their parish during the week. On Saturday night they rush back to be present for Sunday Masses. The bishops find it difficult to deal with this absenteeism. Will such priests not find it very tempting to neglect making visits to communities once teams of OCLs are functioning there?

The problem will increase in the "second generation." The present priests and leaders have the advantage of personally going through the pioneer phase. They have to invent the new structures themselves and therefore own them personally. There is less danger of neglect. But what about the future priests and leaders who find the structure already in existence? Will they find sufficient motivation to maintain it well and to deepen it?

The present priests can rely on having an almost unquestioned authority. Since they are the only ones who can administer the sacraments, people are reluctant to criticise them. This will change when a great number of OCLs can administer the sacraments. Then people can easily criticise the full-time priests or even question the need to receive a visit from them.

In this regard we can learn by observing other Churches. Even Churches which place a high value on lay involvement and on equality, such as the Methodist Church, have made sure that the full-time minister retains strong power. His authority does not rest on the ability to administer sacraments; it is based on other requisites such as the nomination of preachers or the issuing of receipts for Church dues. Is it not obvious that the dioceses which introduce teams of OCLs should from the beginning ensure that there will be a permanent link between them, the full-time priests and the bishop?

Again looking at the experience of other Churches, is it not true that there is a marked difference between the level of in-fighting and splits in those Churches and in the Catholic Church? Is not the reason for this due to the fact that the present monopoly on the sacraments by the full-time priests in the Catholic Church reduces the likelihood of such disputes?

When this monopoly falls away, how will we ensure unity, order, and a regular linkage of the OCL teams with the full-time priest-animator?

There is a definite need to make the priesthood of the OCLs a convincing and attractive institution and to ensure that there is an enduring link between full- and part-time priests.

It will be the task of the bishop and his closest co-workers to ensure that the animator priests have something to offer to the ordained leaders and the communities in the form of retreats, formation, training and planning. When the OCLs become the supplier of the sacraments, the animator priests must be equipped to supply something else and to minister to the communities in other ways.

There is the possibility of giving a special status to the full-time priests, such as appointing each of them (or many of them) as Episcopal Vicar. This recourse will not be necessary in the initial phase of exceptional ordinations of community leaders but it may become meaningful once many communities have their own teams of ordained community leaders. Then the communities will no longer say "we need a priest" but will say "we need unity" and this means they want a clear link to the bishop. Calling the animator priests "vicar of the bishop" will therefore become meaningful as he would exercise part of the overseeing role of the bishop. This presupposes the ability to accompany the OCLs, to unify them, to plan with them and to be the link between them and the bishop.

To counteract absenteeism and to ensure the ongoing motivation of the animator priests the best way is surely to stress the idea of a religious community of diocesan priests where most of them would live together and work in teams. They will plan together and motivate one another to fulfill their new role.

Maintaining unity and order among the ordained community leaders

Maintaining unity, discipline and order in the Church is not something new. The task as regards full-time priests has been difficult enough but easier insofar as offenders could be transferred to other parishes or posts as each one depended economically on the bishop, and as priests do not usually have close relatives among the congregation. These circumstances will not apply to the OCLs.

The many years of study in isolation from his home community weaken the traditional priest's relationship with the community members. Instead he forms ties of friendship with fellow priests. The different life style from the people with whom he

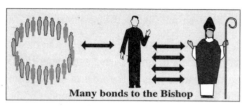

Many bonds to the Bishop

Many bonds to the community

grew up has changed him somewhat so that he has become dissimilar from the people at home and very similar to his fellow clergy. He has become financially dependent on the bishop and knows he can rely on the diocese to an almost unlimited extent for all his needs. The pattern is clear: many bonds to the bishop, few bonds to the parish he serves as illustrated in the first diagram. None of those priests would like to be a priest in his home parish and all would quote the proverb that a prophet is welcome anywhere except in his home community.

The OCLs will live according to a very different pattern and the second diagram shows this: many bonds to the community he serves, few bonds to the diocese. His ties with the community are manifold. His family is there, his relatives, his peers, his business partners and his business competitors. His life story is known as well as all his business dealings. He knows that he will never be the prophet-from-afar but he nevertheless wants to be priest in this home community.

Solutions must be forethought for cases where OCLs can no longer be allowed to continue in their ministry although they insist on doing so. The contingency may arise where the life style of an OCL is no longer compatible with the exercise of the priestly ministry, where his relationship with other OCLs or with the community makes the continuation of his ministry intolerable, or in the less likely event that his teaching deviates from the faith of the Church. If anything of that kind happens and there is no improvement, it has to be made clear to the individual OCL, to the group of OCLs to which he belongs and to the local Christian community that his ministry is for the time being no longer acceptable. Channels for dialogue with the OCL, with the others in his team and with the community have to be established, and ways of arriving at a just and final decision and of enforcing compliance with this must be clearly laid down.

The above eventuality is new insofar as OCLs provide for their livelihood themselves, live on their own premises, cannot be transferred, and have their group of local relatives who will take their side. Cases of tension with the community or with co-workers can therefore not be solved in the traditional way of transfer to another congregation.

Possible ways of preventing community leaders not in communion with the bishop from officiating in the Church

A diocese could introduce the following practice:

Each year every parish arranges a time of renewal for all its leaders, during which the community evaluates its whole life and the performance of the OCLs and other leaders. The Parish Council decides which new candidates for lay ministries should receive formation and at the end of their training who should be commissioned and receive the blessing of leaders from the bishop (or his representative). The Council also determines which active lay leaders are to be presented for the annual rededication and the annual blessing. The rededication of the ordained leaders may take a different form, such as the inclusion of a clause that the Episcopal Vicar must be present in the parish council when the decision is taken to present the OCLs to the bishop. Experience may prompt other procedures. It is when the bishop (or his representative) pays a visit of some days to the parish that these matters are discussed.

At the end of the renewal session the Eucharist is celebrated. The communion of the OCLs with their bishop and the Church is confirmed and a "symbol of priestly communion" exchanged. The community is told:

"The bishop is the centre of the body of priests, called the 'presbyterium'. These your priests exercise the priestly ministry in union with the bishop and with all the priests of the diocese. This gives your whole community the joyful certainty that you live in communion with the whole Church.

Therefore we will now express in a ceremony that the priests of this community are rendering their service in communion with the bishop and the whole Church. If we are united in this way we can be certain that we are in communion with Jesus Christ, the High Priest."

After the explanation the bishop extends a visible sign of communion with the OCLs. Probably it will be wise to introduce a new kind of visible sign, a "symbol of priestly communion," e.g. the "touching of the chalice of the bishop," a special chalice which is kept at the bishop's resi-dence and which the bishop or his representative brings with him at the annual visit and which he invites the OCLs to touch and to drink from during this liturgy as a sign of communion.

The above is one of various ways how communion between the bishop and the OCLs could be expressed and maintained. Other symbolic liturgical actions can be designed for this important ceremony.

If the deliberations which take place during the visit bring to light that one of the OCLs can no longer exercise the priestly ministry at this time, all the aspects of the case are thoroughly discussed by the episcopal vicar/animator priest and the local community who together reach a decision. The OCL may have to be told that he cannot for the time being exercise his priestly ministry although his ordination remains valid. At the final liturgy of that particular year he is not included in the symbol of priestly communion. The way will be kept open for the later re-inclusion of a temporarily suspended priest.

It is necessary to make the moratorium visible to the whole community because the OCL will have many relatives and supporters in his community. The fact that a suspended OCL is not invited to "touch the chalice of the bishop" would serve as a definite and powerful sign that he is not to function as a priest.

Forming one presbyterium to include the various kinds of priest

In the many discussions about the feasibility of introducing viri probati a major objection is that it will lead to two classes of priests. This assertion causes constant confusion because those in favour use the same argument when they call for a diversification of priesthood. The introduction of OCLs will result in a diversification of priesthood and we have to realize that this will be a challenge for the diocese to face. There will not only be two kinds of priest, but several:

Full-time diocesan priests who work as teams of animators;
Full-time diocesan priests who work with special groups or for special tasks;
Priests of religious institutes who work as animator teams;
Diocesan priests or religious priests who serve parishes in the traditional way;
OCLs with little theological formation;
OCLs with a high standard of theological and secular learning;
OCLs living in poverty;
OCLs who are economically well off.

Can we assume that the different kinds of priest can form one presbyterium as demanded by our theological understanding of priesthood? What can we predict with reference to their cooperation and interaction with one another?

Relating well with one another is fairly easy for the present priests who are pretty equal in all respects. They are able to form close friendships and they love to spend time together. Having no family, they have time for each other and can mix

freely. They are immediately welcome in any presbytery. Many of them rest on Mondays, not on Sundays. They all know they are not business people but live from the Church. They know that economically they are fairly equal. They trust each other to a high degree. They have the same education and enjoy the same social status. The Catholic priesthood is a clearly defined social category. They know that they lead an extraordinary but similar life and that they are regarded as ONE group by the faithful and by the world.

Tomorrow this will all change. Some will have a family, others not. A priest cannot just walk into the family of another priest and can no longer mix with all the others as freely as before. There will be vast differences in social status, also between the very poor and the rich, and between the highly and poorly educated OCLs.

A helpful factor will be that the various groupings of priests will spontaneously form themselves into support groups. The religious already have support from within their communities. The members of the newly formed religious community of diocesan priests will fraternize according to their needs. Animators of OCLs may work in teams or affiliate in terms of their office. This will not be a new experience as there already exists a great variety of religious institutes and lay associations in the Church.

Forming a presbyterium is a different matter. The bishop and all the priests make decisions together. It will become very difficult for the whole presbyterium to find a suitable time for meetings because some of its members are in secular employment and have families, which means that their days and hours of work and freedom vary. They will speak diverse  languages and there is a vast disparity in their ability to express themselves. It will be necessary to convene separate meetings to suit the different strata of priests and at the same time to find ways of maintaining links between the groups making up the presbyterium. At intervals a meeting will be convoked where all the priests of a diocese or a deanery can attend.

The episcopal vicars or animator priests assume an important role in creating links between the bishop, the different kinds of priest, the other leaders and the communities.

The task of forming one presbyterium to meet the new vision of Church differs greatly from what has been the practice and it requires much ingenuity but is not impossible. We already see it happening today when we observe large dioceses of Young Churches. They have devised participative processes where the bishop, the priests and many types of lay leaders make decisions together. When a number of the leaders are ordained it should not be too difficult to modify these processes so as to form the presbyterium.

Large diocesan liturgical celebrations are occasions when the presbyterium becomes visible as a unit around the bishop despite the diversity of the priests. However, unity among the priests is primarily and cogently expressed in the small meetings of the OCLs with their animators.

These difficulties and solutions are the real content of the "two classes argument." There is an unreal component of that argument, as if we were splitting into two what must always remain one homogeneous group, or as if we were to create a lower-class appendix to the highly esteemed priests of today.

It is true that we will miss the good old times when there was one homogeneous group of priests, but there is no justification for making the continuation of that advantage our highest priority. Diversity is a basic facet of life and always a challenge; it will be so for the priests as they move into the future but there is no reason why they cannot face it.

The fact that OCLs may change their place of residence in unforeseen ways creates a different kind of challenge for the presbyterium. An OCL may be an employee of a bank whose head office decides to transfer him to another town. He becomes a new member of a parish which knows little or nothing about the existence of OCLs. It could be a parish that discussed the idea of OCLs thoroughly and finally decided against introducing them. Now it suddenly finds one of them in their midst. What rules should be established for cases of this nature when the new parishioner would like to play an active role in the parish?

The same regulations will apply as are already in operation with regard to permanent deacons and to priests who are specialists in certain professions. Such deacons and priests know very well that they will not automatically exercise a pastoral role in another diocese or parish. The OCL follows this simple rule: soon after his arrival he introduces himself to the local priest or bishop as an ordained community leader and declares his readiness to serve the local community in any way it requires. He does not insist on making use of his ordination or even ask to exercise his ministry. He waits patiently until such a request is made to him; meanwhile being as helpful to the community as he can in any other way.

This means that OCLs must be carefully and explicitly prepared for eventualities of this kind. They have received their vocation only in a specific community and will therefore exercise it only in that community. In a corresponding way the bishop, when discerning the candidate's vocation and accepting him for ordination, does so only for this community. The priestly ministry as regards ordained community leaders cannot automatically be exercised in other communities.

We have to accept a difference in the vocation of the OCL and of the full-time priest. The latter receives his vocation for a wider area, for the diocese or for the many places where his religious institute works. The bishop, when admitting him to ordination, undertakes to let him make use of his priesthood where he is needed in the diocese or, in the case of a religious, where he is appointed by his institute. There is no question of his not being able to exercise his ministry. The bishop or superior does not send him to places where he cannot do so.

The community leader is ordained only for his own community. If he emigrates to another community he will need the spiritual strength to continue in his loyalty to the Church, in his personal spirituality and in his allegiance to his new community. He may have to live for some time, perhaps even for several years, without exercising his priesthood. Over the long period of waiting he should not allow himself to become bitter or discouraged. It may take a long time before the receiving diocese, its clergy and the local communities are ready to accept his priestly service. During this time the ordained person may not even be able to celebrate private Masses or exercise any aspect of his ordination. He will nevertheless have to try to be helpful as an active member of the parish in other ways.

Although he cannot practise his ministry he does become a member of the presbyterium of the receiving diocese to some extent because he has introduced himself in the correct way. His membership may have to remain an invisible participation for a certain time but it is nevertheless real.[15]

Serious problems will arise only where an OCL emigrates and does not introduce himself to the receiving diocese or where he even begins exercising his ministry without having been incorporated into its presbyterium. The introduction of OCLs who are economically completely independent opens up this possibility and the need to find ways of dealing with it.

The proper response to these new challenges seems to lie in the emphasis on having not only one new kind of priests, but two new kinds. A diocese which introduces OCLs must at the same time build up within the presbyterium a core group of animator priests who work in close union with the bishop and coordinate the various diocesan and parish structures which require some modification to contain the implementation of OCLs. An important task is the building up of a spirituality in the diocese, which convinces the faithful that there can be no isolated Eucharist and no isolated priesthood. The communities need a faith maturity which enables them to insist on a priesthood which is united with the bishop. Education in this faith maturity includes placing the unity of the Church above personal relationships. It also includes the discernment who has a vocation to and who is faithful to the community-based priesthood we are introducing.

The animator priests are the obvious persons to offer formation and training to the whole community and especially to the parish pastoral council. They are responsible for the theological formation of the OCL candidates and together with other leaders they discern whom the bishop should consider for ordination. They are the resource persons when questions arise as to who is to preside over the sacraments in a certain community and who is not. The bishop cannot be available in so many scattered places;

---

[15]   The "incardination" of OCLs is a different matter and will follow different procedures. Probably it will be wise to retain for the OCLs the existing rule that a migrated priest remains incardinated in the original diocese until agreement has been reached with the receiving diocese. The economically independent OCLs could otherwise find themselves without any sign or sense of belonging.

the animator priests exercise part of the bishop's office of maintaining the unity of the diocese.

There will be a definite need for clear procedures for distinguishing between OCLs who are in communion with the bishop and others who are not. The key persons for those procedures are the animator priests and the parish councils. In areas with poor means of communication the parish councils will need clear rules and reliable skills for dealing with the sudden appearance of persons who offer to preside over the Eucharist but of whom it is not clearly known that they are in communion with the bishop. It could cause untold damage if priesthood would be misused through a lack of precautions. In areas of difficult communications the animator priest cannot be contacted soon and the parish councilors will need the skill and the authority to make prudent decisions on their own. It will be a major task of the animator priests to maintain this ability in all distant parish councils. The realization must be instilled in all communities and especially in all councils that no priest and no OCL can function on his own. It must become clear to all that a priest can act as a priest only if he is in communion with the local bishop and his presbyterium. This will be a vital part of the overall task of formation and training.

Challenges such as these are more apparent today than in the New Testament communities. The single-community dioceses of Ephesus and of Thessalonia had a very small presbyterium whose members were all economically as independent as our OCLs will be and there was surely also some migration in those days, but because of their smaller size there was no need for creating link-priests within the presbyterium in order to ensure its unity. Our larger dioceses will need a presbyterium where two kinds of priest interact. We need two kinds of priest in order to create a united presbyterium.

The reaction of seminarians and the adjustment of seminary formation

The ordination of some leading married men to the ministerial priest-hood and their presiding role in the celebration of the sacraments in certain parishes will be so unfamiliar to most Catholics that the various groups in the Church will mostly adopt a wait-and-see attitude and will therefore not react too strongly in the early phase. We hypothesized their initial responses in a previous chapter. We have to foresee a different kind of reaction occurring some years after the first ordinations, or when the exceptional ordinations have become more numerous.

The seminarians have by that time often discussed the various aspects of having in the future two kinds of priest. They have also heard about the idea of a "religious community of diocesan priests." Even if it is not introduced in the early stages of OCLs, it has to be confirmed that this is the trend of the future. The students' formation will therefore increasingly stress the evolvement of a community-based vision of Church, and will include formation for the new role of the animator priests. Many of the seminarians will see a fulfilling task in this new view of their vocation, one worth sacrificing their whole life for.

The students will also hear rumours circulating in connection with the ordination of married leaders, that this will eventually lead to the so-called "optional celibacy." Seminarians must be helped to discuss such ideas in detail so that they realize that this vision of the Church is a very different one. It is vital for them to see that priesthood based on the evangelical counsels is for the foreseeable future the only kind open to candidates who wish to join the diocesan full-time priests. Seminary staff and the bishop will spend much time in helping the students to understand the deeper vision underlying the introduction of two new kinds of priest. The ordination of OCLs means for the seminarians that the Church will need full-time priests who give their whole life to the cause of evangelization and who will therefore follow the three evangelical counsels (not only one of them).

Awareness of the special vocation to full-time priesthood and how this is implemented in a community-based Church serves several purposes. It prevents idealistic young men from withdrawing from the dioceses to join the religious institutes. It avoids the wrong impression of diocesan priesthood as being something less spiritual than the priesthood of the religious. It negates the false belief that the Church no longer considers complete self-giving and celibacy for the sake of the Kingdom a high value. Awareness raising among the seminarians will also help them to realize that the lone celibate priest of the past has no future. The only type that can survive in the long term is the community-type, living in a group of animator priests. It is important that awareness of all this is disseminated in good time so that seminarians and would-be candidates have a full and true picture of their goal.

The introduction of OCLs means a significant raising of standards for full-time priests and seminarians. It is no longer sufficient that a priest is a faithful administrator of the sacraments. The seminaries have to adapt their formation programme to meet the new requirements. They have also to revise their expectations of the candidates. A candidate for full-time priesthood has to prove his ability to animate and train many part-time priests, to organize and conduct formation programmes, and to devise spiritual programmes for the communities, an ability which cannot be expected from the majority of OCLs.

While we expect this positive reaction among those who have already entered the seminary we also ask ourselves whether the introduction of married OCLs will not mean the end of new entries to the seminary. Probably the new candidates will be fewer, but they will not end completely. When the number of OCLs increases and many parishes have teams of OCLs, there will still be idealistic young people who will feel they could make their contribution by offering their whole life to the Church and to the community. They may feel they could do more than being active in the community and many years later become one of the OCLs. We can assume that there will be young people who feel attracted to become one of the animator priests who regularly come to the parish to the assist the OCLs. What attracts the young people will no longer be "becoming the special person at the altar" or of "being the one person preaching to the masses" but a much deeper role.

In the past the main motive to become a priest came from invitations such as: "you are needed in order to pastor people..." "you are needed to give the sacraments to people". "God needs you to administer his grace to others." This type of invitation will be transformed into a deeper one.

A different type of invitation must go out. "God needs some who can strengthen the brothers and sisters." "God needs people who give their whole life for making the gospel a reality." "God needs priests who can equip and empower the many leaders of the Christian community." "The many leaders of the community need animator priests who can lead others deeper and deeper into the gospel." "We need a group of priests around the bishop, a group which cooperates closely with him in unifying the hundreds of communities and their leaders."

It will be fewer who listen to this more demanding invitation. It is a more complicated invitation. It is a less obvious one. Most probably, therefore, the large scale presence of OCLs will mean a decrease in the number of vocations to full-time priesthood but an increase in their quality.

As the number of OCLs grows and as at the same time the new role of animator priests becomes a reality, the dioceses and their seminaries will adjust their admission policy and their method of formation. Both of these will slowly be adapted in order to ensure that the young priests are almost certainly becoming good animators. The admission policy can of course not easily find indications that the animator talent exists, but it will at least discourage applicants who show indications in their past history and in their character that this ability is probably missing.

The seminary curriculum will also be adjusted in order to equip the future priests for their role as animators and trainers of local leaders. In theory this has already been a goal in some seminaries for many years but not much was done to implement it. When OCLs make their appearance in parishes, when the new role of the animator priests is no longer a hazy ideal but a lived reality, the seminaries will have more courage and more justification to make more real adjustments.

Such adjustments will mean that students will often visit training groups, that students will learn the methodologies of adult learning, that supervised practice sessions of training will be part of the curriculum and that all this will be given a much greater time slot than before, even if it means that the time allocated for academic subjects will have to be reduced.

Once dioceses realize that the quality of formation which the OCLs receive depends largely on the ability of the animator priests to conduct formation, they will not hesitate to adjust the curriculum of the seminaries. The curriculum will, at least in its advanced stage, be adjusted from aiming at what the new priests themselves have to know to what the OCLs have to learn and how the animator priests can help them to learn it.

Seminaries may also adjust their formation by dividing their formation into an initial phase of the usual six years followed three years later by an additional course. Such division has in the past been difficult because the priests could not easily be withdrawn from providing the faithful with pastoral care but it will be more easily possible when OCLs are introduced.

The dioceses will demand such adjustments. They want to make sure that the young priests are definitely able and definitely convinced to fulfill this new role. They will enforce this change even if it leads to a reduction of numbers or to a change of staff in the seminaries.

The dioceses will be motivated to take these steps by several new realizations. They will of course look for efficient animators and for priests who can work in teams. They will also be motivated by the realization that in the distant future there will be much less need for the provider priests of the past. Over and above that, they will even begin to realize that the provider type of priest may in the future be a financial burden to the diocese. Many of the provider priests cannot do much more than the OCLs who receive no remuneration. Moreover it may be exactly those provider priests who may later point out that there is no real difference to the married OCLs and that they should therefore be allowed to get married. They would then ask to receive a family remuneration which is much higher than what the animator priests receive. Fears of this kind will lead the dioceses to adjust seminary formation in such a way that staff and students clearly aim at only one kind of full-time priest, the animator.

There will be people who begin suggesting that the formation process should be changed altogether. They will say the future formation process should be "first vir probatus priest then animator priest." This is certainly a possibility but it should not be enforced. It can evolve gradually as a parallel access for becoming a member of the religious community of diocesan priests. All will then depend on the extent to which this parallel route proves to be a success and it will take many years before this can be seen clearly. Until then the seminaries will have to continue even if they become smaller in size.

Such a parallel alternative formation could perhaps be tried in this way: a young person who feels called to be an animator priest works actively in a parish while exercising a profession. He attaches himself to a team of animator priests and through them to the youth group of the religious community of diocesan priests. Such a youth group meets regularly for spiritual formation and for some theological study but its members continue to live from their secular profession. After some years they may even reside together. Theological study is gradually intensified but remains part-time study. During this time the young candidates already take part in the training sessions of the local OCLs and they work closely with them in the parish. Ordination to the diaconate and even as one of the OCLs is possible even at this stage, depending on the circumstances. Full membership in the religious community of diocesan priests, full-time study, and the giving up of the secular profession should, however, only follow at a stage when it is clear that the person can make a permanent commitment and has the ability to work as an animator priest.

A formation process of this kind is certainly not impossible and will appear more feasible once OCLs are introduced. It could also prove a much more natural and genuine way of training animator priests. It is, however, an untried method and should not be quickly suggested as a replacement for the seminaries. It is much better to begin with an adjustment of the present seminary system.

Religious institutes and the changes in priesthood

In most dioceses of the Young Churches of today the priests of religious institutes constitute a large percentage. During the period of introducing married *viri probati* priests, due to the many uncertainties, the institutes may lose some members, but not a significant percentage. We can assume that most of their members will be very willing to join the efforts to make this new vision a reality. Their continued life and witness of total dedication will be highly appreciated during this difficult period and will reduce the painful impact of uncertainty and change in many dioceses. In dioceses where, during the period of change, affairs threaten to get completely out of hand, religious priests can provide stability.

Some dioceses may ask the institutes to take over more tasks because married OCLs are not acceptable in certain areas. Commentators have expressed the fear that should the religious institutes become the only reliable group they will automatically yield power, even to the extent of exceeding that of the bishop. It is possible that they will help out in areas where OCLs cannot be introduced but it is unlikely that they can expand to any degree. They will serve as a stable factor in the midst of change, but not as an overpowering force.

While the dioceses will try to be quick in adjusting their seminary formation so that it will dissuade those who want to become provider priests, the religious institutes may be slower in this adjustment. The reason for this difference is that those dioceses which are well prepared for the ordination of OCLs in all their parishes will realize that the ordination of priests who cannot be animators may become a big financial burden for them and yet will not be useful for the diocese. Some of the religious institutes do not have to foresee this development to the same extent because they can transfer the provider-type of priests to other places. They can therefore more easily afford to continue with a more traditional type of formation. Even those institutes which work in dioceses that have OCLs will realize that for many decades to come there will be other dioceses who do not have OCLs and will therefore ask religious institutes to supply the traditional kind of priests.

The recruitment and formation of young members for religious institutes will, however, be influenced by the dramatic changes in the seminaries of the dioceses. They will realize that their own priests will be asked more and more to work as animators and they want to be prepared for that task. The transformation of their formation will therefore move in a similar direction but at a slower pace.

It is probably correct to assume that the introduction of OCLs and the new overall vision which this implies will be helpful to the religious institutes. It will change the atmosphere under which they invite new members. What will it mean for young people when they see secular people presiding as priests every Sunday? We should not too easily assume that the young people will now lose interest in religious communities. We should not assume that they will say: "Now there is no need to become a full-time diocesan priest or a Franciscan or a Dominican. I can get to the altar as an average Christian." They may well be helped by this new religious experience to detect some deeper reasons for joining religious Communities.

The introduction of OCLs will mean the bridging of the wide gap between laity and clergy, between those "cared for" and those "caring for." It will reduce the impression of a "closed caste" which alone holds power in the Church and which alone has sacred authority. It will make the Church more transparent. It will help religious institutes to show more clearly their true nature as communities of people who are totally committed to the gospel.

The financial implications of ordaining community leaders.

The ordination of community leaders does not of itself mean any financial burden for the dioceses since OCLs receive no remuneration at all. Even a large number would not cause expenses; this would reduce the cost of frequent travel to distant places to celebrate the sacraments. Anglican dioceses who have introduced OCLs point out that this structure is far less expensive because it requires fewer full-time priests. Their Church statistics indicate a possible ratio of the two categories of priests. In one diocese of 160 priests only 30 are full-time, supported by the diocese, while the others are self-supporting priests who work without remuneration. In other dioceses there are 30 self-supporting priests among a total of 80, or similar percentages. [16]

---

[16]   Figures of 1992, Archdiocese of Pretoria, South Africa, and from other Anglican dioceses.

What dioceses may well fear is that some community leaders, ordained as voluntary workers, may later complain that they are overburdened and ask to be remunerated. This can be avoided. Firstly, by ordaining not individuals but always teams, we greatly reduce the likelihood of such happenings. Secondly, the suitable procedures have already been demonstrated with regard to the permanent deacons who are self-supporting. Before they are ordained they make a written declaration that they will never rely on remuneration. Finally, a further reference to the Anglican dioceses shows that various preconditions to prevent such requests have proved efficient. [17]

There is the apprehension that although OCLs may not of themselves cause increased financial burdens in the foreseeable future, dioceses in later decades could be faced with a financial problem. The presence of OCLs in a diocese could later lead to more requests by full-time priests to be allowed to continue as married priests which would mean that they need an increased financial support. To address this fear it is necessary to introduce new principles:

A new principle: ordination as such does not imply remuneration

Those ordained as local community leaders enter into an agreement with the diocese that they will at no time expect financial assistance or sustenance from it, not even in times of need, unemployment or sickness. Canon Law (c.281 §3) stipulates that deacons who follow a civil profession are to see to their own and to their family needs from their income. Before ordination to priesthood, a community leader should make a similar statement that he expects no financial assistance.

People may find this difficult to understand. They are so used to the fact that every ordained person is financially completely dependent on the Church that they find it inadmissible for an ordained local leader not to be in a position to claim financial support, not even when he is in

---

[17] In the Anglican Archdiocese of Pretoria a self-supporting priest who wishes to become a full-time remunerated priest can only do so after undergoing years of additional studies.

need. The new principle becomes acceptable when we remember the fact that active parishes rely on the voluntary work of hundreds of lay people and none of them would dream of claiming support from the Church in times of need. When some of them are ordained this does not change their financial position. Spontaneous assistance in times of need can of course be offered but cannot be claimed and has never been claimed by voluntary leaders.

The principle is much easier to understand and to implement when OCLs are ordained as teams, not as individuals. If only one person is ordained and later gets into need, there is a greater possibility of people thinking that he has a right to financial assistance. It will be difficult to prevent such assistance from developing into employment. It is therefore important to state from the beginning the principle that ordination by itself does not imply any remuneration.

A new principle: If agreements are changed, obligations change

With regard to the present celibate priests there is no need to foresee a future financial problem. We can assume that the majority of the present priests continue serving as they have done. If after 50 or a 100 years the Church were to accept some married full-time priests, they will be relatively few in number and will not cause an impossible financial burden. Provided OCLs are introduced with a sound structure, then most priestly functions are fulfilled by unremunerated priests and only a minority of the priests work as highly trained, remunerated, full-time animators, the majority of whom live as members of a religious community of diocesan priests. We do not envisage for that time or the more distant future any large-scale request by celibate priests to marry. The number is not expected to exceed the general trend of the pre-OCL stage and should not cause a sudden financial impasse. If in some countries a somewhat higher number of celibate priests is induced by the changes in priesthood to insist on getting married, new principles have to come into play to reduce the financial impact. The key idea is that the change of agreements requires on both sides a change in obligations.

The present agreement concluded with the celibate, full-time priest is that on his side he will never change his profession, and on the side of the Church that she will support him under all circumstances connected with his work. The ordination to the priesthood under the present canon law implies an agreement with the priests for a "remuneration that befits their condition" and "it is to be such that it provides for the necessities of their life" (c.281 §1), not a remuneration which enables them to provide for a family. The agreement rests on the presupposition that the priests have decided to remain celibate and therefore only have to provide for the needs of their own life. If it should happen that this presupposition one day falls away because the Church in some areas has reason to accept that some priests cannot continue their celibate life, the obligations necessarily change on both sides. The diocese is not obliged to increase remuneration to sustain a family, and the priest is no longer obliged to work full-time for the diocese should he decide to marry and take up civil employment in order to provide for his newly established family.

Not all priests who marry will then continue working full-time for the diocese

Should such situations develop, the original contract necessarily ceases. A new agreement can be drawn up between the diocese and the priest concerned, not a general agreement that applies to all cases. Each case has to be treated on its own merits.

The diocese has to consider carefully whether it does need the full-time service of the particular priest after he marries, and whether it has the means to give a remuneration which provides for a family. It can then enter a new agreement with him, but it is not obliged to do so. The diocese needs regional animators besides the teams of OCLs and is free to seek them among the celibate who need less remuneration or among the married priests. Circumstances and means determine the choices each diocese makes.

If the diocese considers that a particular priest who wants to get married is not able to take up the work of a full-time regional animator or to do more than what the team of OCLs does, then it is not obliged to enter an agreement which includes family remuneration.

The same freedom to enter new agreements must be given to the priest. If he considers that the remuneration which the diocese can offer is not meeting his and his wife's expectations, he is free to choose a civil profession. He can then continue doing priestly work in his spare time as the OCLs do. This will avoid the present bitter reactions which follow when a priest who gets married has to give up all priestly work.

It will be difficult to do complete justice to the priests who during that time will choose to get married. It may happen that the diocesan authorities feel compassion for a number of their priests who no longer feel able to keep their promise of celibacy, made under different circumstances. Their sympathetic understanding does not give the priests a right to marry; it contains only a certain possibility. The diocese is not obliged to provide family support; there is merely a possibility of doing so. Both the diocese and the priests have to be considerate, especially where a diocese has very limited financial means.

Church structures have always been based on numerous sacrifices made by the communities and their pastors. The community of believers does not want to operate like a business concern. The call to make sacrifices is not just an accidental one but one of essence. Even when regulations and circumstances change, all of us will continue to make sacrifices and to rely on the sacrifices made by others.

Dangers to be avoided when introducing ordained community leaders

We have observed that many proponents of the ordination of community leaders say they foresee no serious problems connected with this step. However, the history of the Catholic Church and the experience of other Churches prove that such an innovation can go wrong and cause much damage to the Church. Several of these dangers have been pointed out at various places throughout the above pages. They are now briefly reviewed.

The danger of a new type of clericalism

The chief danger to be avoided is that of a clericalistic type of viri probati priests who will later hinder the development of the vision of a community-based Church which is the only one that has a future in modern society, a Church which is a community and which is at the service of the world around us.

Clericalism is not easy to define but there are certain symptoms by which people diagnose this disease. It is not an unavoidable disease and not all members of the clergy contract it. It was diagnosed in many members of the present clergy and the danger surely exists that even the OCL could fall victim to it. The fact that OCLs lead lay people's lives is no safe antidote against it. Clericalism is even today pointed out in many non-ordained lay leaders.

It will be the task of those who design the mode of operation of OCLs to reduce the temptations to clericalism and to increase the antidotes. Some of the proven antidotes against clericalism are team work, rotation of office, avoidance of privileges, collaboration as equals with non-ordained leaders, regular evaluation among the leaders, regular evaluation with the whole community and above all reflection on the New Testament.

Even the following brief sections on monopoly and on remuneration have to do with the danger of clericalism.

The danger of a monopoly by one community leader

Where only one community leader is ordained in a parish which has always been passive, an undesirable monopoly can arise. The congregation remains just as passive as it was, and may be tempted to become more so, since they now have a person whom they expect to do everything for them. It is this danger which is most commonly overlooked. Practically all Catholic publications which advocate the ordination of viri probati are asking for the ordination of only one person per community, and none seems to see any danger in this procedure.

While we Catholics have no experience in this regard we can learn from the experience of other Churches which have already tried to put one voluntary pastor in charge of each parish. What was the frequent result? It was not as we might have expected. The community did not try to lighten the burden of this one generous voluntary pastor but often they did the opposite. The community tried to collect funds so that the voluntary pastor could become a full-time pastor. Their main motive was to become a "respectable" congregation which managed to have more than a second-rate pastor but a real one, a full-time one.

This desire came even from poorer congregations from whom we might have expected the opposite reaction. It is clear that such congregations could only afford financial support of one full-time pastor and would therefore make sure he remained the only candidate. In other cases the desire to transform the voluntary pastor into a full-time one may well come not from the side of the congregation but from the side of the voluntary pastor who feels overburdened and asks to become a full-time worker. To reenforce his wish he will of course make sure that he remains the only candidate.

At the same time this kind of monopolizing ministry is unattractive to parishioners who have charisms, especially younger members who find such a Church unsatisfactory and outdated.

The possibility of the OCLs becoming monopolistic community leaders is not prevented by mere exhortations directed to them or to the congregation, but only by an approach which bases the whole life of the parish on community building.

The danger of linking ordination with remuneration

If the mistake is made to give ordained community leaders some remuneration, then there can be only one OCL in most congregations, especially in developing countries. This increases the danger of monopolism with the result of making people even more passive, of tempting the leaders to insist on their function, of leaders stressing their authority and relying less on their ongoing formation, of favouring an outdated type of leaders, and on other consequences of monopoly as described above.

A similar danger arises if, instead of a remuneration, we allow presents, gifts, benefits, privileges or similar acknowledgments. A system of gift-giving discourages team-work; the more community leaders there are, the fewer the gifts each receives. It inhibits the sharing of tasks freely among the many unremunerated lay leaders. Practices of this nature are unhealthy.

There may be cases where remuneration is unavoidable, but these must remain rare exceptions.

The danger of ordaining community leaders where there is no animator to accompany them

Where the ordination of leaders is motivated only by the scarcity of the sacraments, there may be little emphasis on their ongoing formation. Without it there is real danger of OCLs assuming a monopolistic style, adopting wrong leadership attitudes, and of performing in an old-fashioned, outdated manner. This may lead to their exercising a negative influence in the presbyterium of the diocese to which they belong by virtue of their ordination.

If ordained leaders are not accompanied, there is the risk of their becoming isolated priests. This is not our gospel-based vision of priesthood and it is unlikely that they can continue to serve the community well over any length of time. When tensions arise between an isolated ordained leader and the community or when the continued exercise of priesthood becomes impossible for other reasons, it is difficult to find a peaceful solution.

A dangerous situation could arise in areas where many community leaders are ordained without being linked through a structure of animator priests. Without a clearly structured, regular system of ongoing formation assessment and planning, it is most likely that the large number of OCLs will gradually lose fervour, will decline in standards, will get locked in disagreements, will lose acceptance by their communities. The sacramental tradition of the Church could lose its dignity. If such a situation would continue for a few years it will be difficult for a bishop to rectify it.

The danger of introducing the new kind of priests without giving the present priests a new role

As we have seen above in the chapter on the new role of full-time priests, when the new type of *viri probati* priests is being introduced, the new role of the animator priests must also be considered. If this is not done, the present priests may lose their idealism. A new vision of Church must include a new vision for the existing priests.

Again, it would be fatal to adopt a wait-and-see attitude. It is wrong just to demand the ordination of local leaders, saying the resulting dangers would be dealt with when they arise. Leading the existing priests into a situation of uncertainty could result in many defections from the priesthood and in a general loss of generosity and loyalty. This would be difficult to rectify.

The thousands of priests of today have made their life commitment for the sake of a great ideal. That ideal is actually not put in question, but if the wrong impression is created – as if this ideal were now abandoned – this could endanger the self-giving of many of the existing priests. It is our duty to make it very clear from the beginning that the original ideal remains. It is only the roles which are changing and the existing priests do certainly have a key role in future. We owe it to them and to the whole Church to make this new role clear.

Questions a diocese should consider before initiating the process

The above pages have shown that it cannot be a question of just filling a few gaps by ordaining some additional providers of sacraments. Dioceses therefore have to consider whether they are prepared to aim at the new vision underlying the ordination of local leaders. If they are not able to do so, they should wait until they are in the position to take this step.

Each diocese will therefore have to reflect carefully whether it is really ready to start making this move. What questions should the dioceses ask themselves?

The first question is probably that of unity. A change of this magnitude should not be attempted by a bishop and his priests if they have not managed to reach a stage where they can talk fairly openly with each other, can trust each other quite well and have proved that they can solve problems by working together. There are of course different opinions in any group, different characters and some who always love to dissent. This is not disunity. Disunity means organized and militant opposition groups. Disunity means there is insufficient will to come to a consensus. Disunity of this kind means a stage where the group, when faced by a problem, frequently ends up either by doing nothing at all, or by letting things go wrong, or by escalating the conflict to teach others a lesson, or in similar deadlocking mechanisms. A diocesan presbyterium of this type cannot begin a change of the magnitude of introducing OCLs. A certain measure of unity and cooperation is a prerequisite.

When this basic unity exists, a diocese could begin dialog sessions in which the overall vision is considered. Lists of preconditions for the diocese and for parishes similar to the ones offered above can then help the presbyterium to see whether it can move further ahead.

The study of such lists may lead to questions such as these:

1. Are we prepared to present a new vision, not just a new legislation? Can we present at one and the same time the idea of teams of OCLs and of teams of animator priests? Can we present the new role of the existing priests in order to motivate them to continue with their total self-giving as celibate priests?

2. Will we be able to separate the proposal to introduce OCLs from the issue of women's ordination?

3. Do we accept a mixed presbyterium? As we indicated above, the presbyterium of the future will comprise several kinds of priest. Some may find the pluriformity unwelcome but it cannot be avoided. When introducing OCLs we must accept this change as a necessary component of the process. It can mean an enrichment.

Only if a fair consensus can be reached on questions of this kind can the diocese succeed if it decides to move ahead. If the joint determination can not be reached to walk this road together, it is better to wait. If a fair consensus exists, the bishop and the priests can deal with further practical questions such as these:

4. What must be included in the "list of preconditions" to be published in the diocese so that the parishes and groups of the diocese can debate the possible introduction of OCLs? How will the fulfilment of the preconditions be checked when parishes apply for the ordination of some of their community leaders?

5. How will we react to the questions of seminarians? Who will make the contacts?

6. How will we react to priests who insist on getting married during the time of transition?

7. How will parishes be invited to dialogue with all their people before introducing OCLs? How will the parish teams be trained for conducting the dialogue sessions?

8. What kind of training do we suggest for OCLs? Can we leave this to be solved differently in the regions? Or do we need guidelines? Is it helpful to suggest group-conducted liturgies as a preparatory step?

There will, of course, be many other aspects which dioceses will have to consider before initiating the process of introducing OCLs, but the above ones have been listed in order to make us aware that dioceses should not act in a hasty way.

In preparation for a decision, three viewpoints: NOW - NEVER - LATER

In the not too distant future, a decision has to be taken by the highest authority of the Church as to whether or not to allow the careful introduction of the ordination of community leaders. In preparation for this final decision study meetings need to be held, symposia and seminars in order to consider the arguments for and against. There should be meetings of experts, meetings of councils, meetings of organizations, meetings of bishops and mixed meetings, in order to prepare the final decision.

The previous pages have tried to clarify what is at stake and suggest processes to follow the decision. We can now allow our fantasy to picture some of the discussions which will take place.

Three main groups of opinions will emerge. Let us call them the "NOW group" because some want the permission to be given right now; the "NEVER group" of those who are totally against the suggestion; and the "LATER group" who see some merit in it but think the time for its introduction has not yet come.

As a member of the group which has initiated the session, one of the "NOW" group opens the debate:

> I speak for those who ask that in certain circumstances the ordination of proven men be permitted by the Church. We have already presented our suggestions in great detail. They can be summed up by the key expressions "ordaining teams of community leaders" and "beginning with a limited number of exceptions".

> The motivations for the proposal are manifold. I ask you to note that as the primary motive I do not mention the scarcity of the present priests, but rather the wish to give fuller participation to all members of the Church. Other important motives are to build self-reliant, mature communities and to narrow the gap between the communities and their ordained leaders. The last, but nevertheless urgent motive, is to overcome the scarcity of the sacraments.

> I also wish to point out that included in the deliberations we have put before you is the assurance that it will be possible to introduce the ordination of proven leaders without endangering the continued faithful service of the present priests. It means an enormous step, but a step which enriches the Church. I ask the assembly to accept the proposal.

One of the NEVER group replies:

We have heard the previous speaker putting his proposal to us in the name of many others and especially in the name of the millions of Catholics who presently endure the painful situation of being served by too few priests. We admire the careful coverage of all aspects of the issue and the precise way in which the details have been compiled. We are especially grateful for the painstaking efforts made to foresee ways of preserving the spirit of dedication among the priests who presently serve our Church.

In the name of many others I now wish to explain why we are convinced that the Church should never, never embark on this path. The proposal is presented as a solution, but it is no solution.

A solution, according to the meaning of the term, should solve the problem. This proposal tries to solve several problems. We have listened carefully and have heard that it is intended to solve not only the issue of the scarcity of priests but also other Church concerns. Firstly, the proposal will not solve those problems; secondly, it will create several new and even more serious problems.

The proposal aims at changing the life-nerve of the Church, the ministerial priesthood, and thereby to solve all the problems mentioned. The life-nerve of the Church is just as delicate as the nerves of our body. Tampering with it is likely to destroy it. The nervous system of our human body has evolved under God's creating hands over millions of years to become the marvelous and complicated system it is today and we hardly understand it, let alone are we able to improve it.

The same is true of the Catholic priesthood. We know that it has evolved over twenty centuries. Yes, it was somehow different in the beginning. Yes, there were married priests and there were viri probati priests who followed their secular profession as tentmakers and fishermen and other secular professions. But then Catholic priesthood developed a different trend until it became what we have today. To tamper with it is dangerous.

Celibate, full-time priesthood has evolved and has proved its worth. Church historians tell us in great detail how difficult it was to reach the desired goal, to establish the present discipline of priests. It is too dangerous to reverse the development of those centuries.

The proposal envisages two kinds of priest instead of the present one kind. It takes care to demonstrate to us that the establishment of the new kind will not endanger the old kind. But how much proof do we have of that promise? The explanations offered are rather vague. Yes, the proposal suggests ways of avoiding total chaos, including procedures to avoid the loss of total dedication of the celibate priests. We acknowledge the effort that has gone into all this but none of it contains solid proof. Things can just as well go very differently from what has been projected.

It may very well be that the final result of your proposal will look very similar to optional celibacy. We see that you have carefully avoided the phrase "optional celibacy," but what you suggest as the future diversity of priesthood comes very close to it. It is not your immediate objective, but it will be the ultimate outcome – and this must never happen. I ask the assembly to reject this proposal.

A NOW proponant clarifies their position:

Let me explain in a simple way why the phrase "optional celibacy" is unsuitable for this debate. The phrase is too close to the many unimportant "optional extras" between which we are choosing in daily life. When we buy a car, when we choose between different models of machines, we are told we can take or leave certain "optional" features and these are always the minor choices, not the major ones.

It is clear to everybody that in our case of priesthood we are dealing with a major choice in life, with the acceptance of a vocation. We are not dealing with a minor matter. We are dealing with two kinds of priestly vocations, the vocation of ordained community leaders and the vocation of animator priests. One is called either to this vocation or to the other. One is not "opting" between the two. This is why the term 'optional celibacy' is simply not suitable for this debate.

Our proposal encourages the existing priests to remain faithful to their vocation and to discover it even more deeply than before. It is no threat for the priests of today. It is not a step back but a step forward. It does not propose less spirituality but more.

One of the NEVER group still sees a danger in these ideas:

The intention of the previous speaker is to make us feel safe and secure. However, in the study publications, there are passages which show clearly that among the animator priests a certain small number of exceptions might be tolerated at a later stage. They may not be intended, but they will be permitted. If a married, ordained community leader shows that he can become a good animator, he will not be rejected. Such exceptions will not be permitted during the first years but are possible later, it is said.

The reality is that in this particular matter one cannot work with exceptions. A discipline such as our present priesthood can only be kept by all, or it will disintegrate. What you envisage will lead to a creeping decay of our present discipline. We can only keep it universally, or abandon it. If a diocese starts with allowing one exception, it will be forced to agree to the second one. Dioceses will have to follow on with tens and then with hundreds.

The only solution is to retain our present discipline.

A NOW member offers clarification:

"Please let me clarify the point made that the dioceses 'will be forced to follow on with tens and hundreds.' Such a deplorable development could happen if we were to introduce the ordination of community leaders without offering a new role to the existing priests. This building up of a new role for the existing priests is therefore a key element of our proposal. It is this element which will avoid what the previous speaker rightly fears.

Our proposal should be seen not as the abandoning of an ideal, but rather as the introduction of a new ideal, a new vision. It is the vision of a higher form of participation in the communities. It is an ideal for which we can invite the existing priests to make increased efforts, not less. It is, as we said, not a step back but a step forward.

Let me add that in the course of time the proposal will actually lead to a higher standard of priests. Today the dioceses are so short of priests that sometimes the bishop is tempted to say yes to ordain where he actually feels he should say no. The sheer need of any priest forces him almost to think 'better a weak one than none,' because people are starved of the sacraments.

This will be different if our proposal is accepted. A diocese will have a sufficient number of priests who can celebrate the sacraments in the parishes. When it comes to the ordination of animator priests, the diocese can then afford to be more selective. It will take only those who have the spirituality needed for that kind of priestly role.

Far from leading to a 'decay' of priestly spirituality, the proposal actually leads to a higher motivation.

A member of the LATER group asks to be heard:

The previous speaker correctly points out that the proposal to ordain married proven leaders does not envisage the introduction of married, full-time priests and that it contains appropriate measures to safeguard the dedication of the present priests. All in this house appreciate these two very valid assertions and we associate ourselves with the aim of the proposal.

There are genuine gospel values in the proposal and this has perhaps been overlooked by the earlier speaker. Those values must be pursued. The question is how and when. Can they be pursued now as proposed, and can they be pursued in the very way of the proposal? This is where we and many others in the Church have doubts.

Is our time suitable for this proposal? What will happen in our times if we accept this proposal today?

The proposal continually mentions that most communities and most dioceses are not ready for the change and suggests effective ways of preparing for it, also of rectifying developments that might happen to go wrong. These dangers are foreseen even by those who make the proposal.

Is it not much better to wait for some time until the conditions are more conducive to such a profound change which is in itself quite acceptable and even desirable?

I therefore propose that the Church should, immediately and with great vigour, embark on developing community spirit and lay ministries. If after some years we see satisfactory progress in this regard, then we will again debate the proposal presented to us today.

A NOW member responds:

What is it really that calls for an immediate acceptance of our proposal? Over the past decade many theologians and authors have repeatedly stressed the negative consequences of allowing the present situation to continue. Their greatest emphasis has been on the dire results if in so many parts of the world Catholics become used to celebrating Sunday without Holy Mass and to seeing laymen perform tasks which have always been regarded as requiring ordained ministers. This is an erosion of the sacramental structure of our faith. It has been going on for a long time already and it should not be allowed to continue. Now is the time to act.

A speaker of the NEVER group disagrees:

We are aware of the negative effects of the situation to which the previous speaker refers, but we also foresee the very nega-

tive effects of the proposal. A solution can be found only by recourse to the proven methods and principles, by praying for vocations and by utilizing all present resources to deepen the faith.
The decline of vocations has been a phenomenon of a relatively
short period, of the last 50 years, and we cannot say it will continue indefinitely. The kind of priesthood we have did not develop within a short time but over many centuries. We cannot
sacrifice that long development by rushing into something quite
unknown.

The LATER group maintains its position:

We need more time for study and consideration before we
embark on such a dramatic change from which there is no return. We know that the matter is urgent, that the present shortage of priests is having an adverse effect in the congregations,
but our problem is the utter finality of the proposed diversification of priesthood. We must have more time to ensure that the
communities are properly prepared as we have said earlier, and
time to come to terms with all the details of the proposal. We
are grateful for the studies that have been undertaken so far, but
more are required before we undertake the decisive step proposed to us. We cannot accept the proposal at this moment.

A NOW group member counters:

"I wish to remind my brothers and sisters of some details
presented to you. The proposal stipulates that teams of ordained
community leaders can be introduced only where for a long period of time, for several years, the readiness of the communities,
their leaders and their priests has been demonstrated. A list of
preconditions for dioceses and for parishes, of which we have
included samples in our proposal, are considered mandatory to
prevent the introduction of viri probati where a diocese or parish
is unprepared. Therefore it is totally impossible that the process
could take place where the diocese and the parish is not ready
for it. To await a time when practically all parishes would have
reached the required stage of preparedness would mean to frus-

trate utterly those who are ready now. Throughout the entire world we see signs of this wholesome desire for participation and we have often regarded this yearning of the people as one of the signs of our times. It should not be left unanswered. Those who are ready to introduce viri probati should be allowed to do so now; others follow when they are likewise prepared.

And another NOW adds:

I support the last speaker. Waiting too long can lead to a disastrous emergency situation. If the loss of a sacramental sense among Catholics becomes increasingly felt, then a stage can be reached when the whole Church is ready to act out of pressure. The authorities will then not follow the gradual process we have suggested but will proceed immediately to make the sacraments more available. The sudden introduction of a new kind of priest is a wrong process and it will be almost impossible to rectify. We have to introduce a new kind of priest step by step. Therefore we should not wait any longer. We should begin carefully, but we should begin now."

The NEVER side introduces a new aspect into the debate:

Our present priests need all their courage to stand up to the chaos of our modern world. They should be strengthened in this heroic effort, not distracted by an unpredictable experiment. The issue we face today is the enormous confusion of modern thinking. It is not the time to tamper with the proven structures of the Church. As somebody has said in a metaphor: the hurricane is not the time to try to improve the roof.

The proposal will increase the confusion instead of confronting it. We should be united in our stance against the present degeneration, but the proposal destroys unity and it diverts our attention from the real issues. It will weaken the priesthood and the Church. It cannot be accepted.

A NOW interprets this problem in a different way:

The metaphor of the hurricane was phrased twenty five years

ago, 1971 during the first debate on *viri probati* ordinations, and the storm is still continuing. There is no end in sight. It is not a passing hurricane but the headwind against which the Church will have to struggle all the time. To wait until it passes does not help.

Yes, we have to face up to our confused world. We can do so only as a Church which has credibility in the eyes of the people of today. We have to listen to our people and give effect to their desire to participate in the life of the Church. What we propose will not weaken the Church; on the contrary, it will enhance it. To strengthen our priests and our communities cannot mean to reject all change, to refuse adapting all that has developed over the centuries to our time. An inflexible Church fails in credibility because it fails to face the modern world. We constantly hear from concerned people that one of the greatest needs of our communities is to be enabled to share their charisms and to give an example of acting together. This is what our proposal aims at.

The LATER group places their hope elsewhere:

Strong medicine with risky side-effects should be taken only when it has become clear that this is the only way left. This proposal should therefore be accepted only when it is clear that there is no hope of solving the shortage of priests through an increase of vocations or through a redistribution of the existing priests. In Africa, in Latin America and in parts of Asia vocations are on the rise. The outcome of this development must be seen first before we embark on the proposed step. The proposal is well thought out, but it still entails certain risks. We must remain on safe ground as long as possible.

This argument, too, is offset by a NOW follower:

We have remained on the path of the present ministry structure for a long time and have seen the negative effects in an ever increasing way. To continue on it any longer cannot be called a safe option. Many people have described in great detail the negative consequences of remaining on this path any longer. It surely involves a great risk – just as our proposal involves a certain risk. We are not comparing a safe path with a risky one. No, we are comparing two paths both of which involve risk, but we believe that there is much greater risk in maintaining the status quo."

A NEVER speaker again takes a more general, negative view:

The proposal comes from good intention but is unrealistic in several ways. It is unrealistic to assume that a majority of the existing priests will become animators, will not be weakened by the introduction of ordained viri probati but will even become more firmly dedicated. Realistic predictions will tell us rather that this proposal will mean a weakening of dedication for the majority and it will therefore lead to uncertainty and to a loss of discipline among the priests.

The proposal is also unrealistic in assuming that we have a majority of bishops who can lead their priests through the process which is proposed. It is more realistic to assume that the majority of bishops would be overwhelmed by the magnitude of this change and would be unable to guide it in the way which is proposed.

It is further unrealistic to assume that in a majority of parishes we can find teams of deeply convinced, reliable candidates for the formation of teams of viri probati priests, together with fervent communities whom we expect to suddenly embrace community building and support teams of ordained leaders. One cannot presume such an ideal development.

A final unrealistic presumption is that after all these changes there will still be vocations for becoming full-time animator priests who live the evangelical counsels. It is more realistic to assume that a development of this kind will lead to a virtual end of vocations. The public and the youth will simply be prompted to demand having a majority of full-time married priests as the other Churches have.

To sum up, the realistic result of this proposal will be that the Catholic Church would abandon its unique kind of priesthood and would simply follow the type of ministry the other Churches have. It might retain a tiny percentage of monastic priests as is left over in the Anglican Church but that will mean nothing more than a rare exception. The realistic prediction is that the proposal will make our Church a place of disunity, of disciplinary chaos and of confusion – not at all a sign to the world. For these reasons the proposal cannot be accepted.

A NOW proponant responds to this challenge:

Realism is indeed what we need, not wild guesses or exaggerations. There are ways of making predictions – on both sides – which are realistic and there is the temptation to make wild guesses and to exaggerate in order to defeat the other side – again on both sides. What we need is careful, honest study of the facts we have. There are aspects of this question on which we have no facts at all. Let us admit it openly. There are aspects where all we have is certain indications, then it is our task to describe them correctly. This is respect for reality, true realism. Both the hopes and the fears need realism. This is our task now, to critically and realistically examine the signs of hope and of danger. We have to carefully examine the indications of what could happen through our YES or through our NO.

Exaggeration offers itself as a weapon to both sides, each one painting the other in the worst possible scenario. One can of course sketch the proposed introduction of ordained community leaders in the worst possible way. The same is possible of the opposite. What will happen if the Church remains inflexible can also be pictured in a deeply frightening way. One can just as well predict in a shocking way that the Church will fail to be a sign of hope to the world if it continues with the narrow ministry structure it presently has.

The proposal was put to you in a way which tried to be as realistic as possible. When you studied it you saw again and again that it tries to build only on predictions based on what

appears possible, not more. It tries to build on facts and developments which are already a reality. It tries to show that this is
the more promising path into the future and this is why it should
be accepted.

Another of the NEVER group again takes up the topic of realism:

The proposal is designed as the high road of fully dedicated,
celibate animator-priests and of dioceses which are fully convinced
of the idea of self-ministering communities. They are all determined to overcome the stage of the provider-priest. This is how
they may start, but then exceptions will be made: some married
lay-animators will be accepted as full-time priests, though this
was originally not intended; then some animator priests will get
married and will be allowed to continue, although this was not
the original plan. They continue first under the name of animator-priests but eventually operate as provider-priests. Finally some
very promising young men will ask to be trained as full-time
married priests saying they want to become very good animators.
They should not be accepted, says the proposal, but the bishop
is in trouble and thinks they will become good animators. This is
what they say but actually they want to work as provider-priests,
and how can you stop them once they are ordained? These three
access roads to full-time married provider-priesthood are not intended in the high road proposal. However, these exceptions will
occur in our non-ideal dioceses. That high road will widen, it will
become easier and will become lower. What started as exceptions will become widespread praxis. We will then be back to the
provider priests but with a difference: they will by then be a
confusing mixture of married and celibate priests, of full-timers
and part-timers. It will all end up as the low road of optional
celibacy which was not intended. In other words the proposal is
too ideal and will not remain on that ideal level.

It is of course envisaged that this possibility should be discussed during the dialog stage and steps should be agreed upon
to avoid it. However, in many dioceses it is difficult to reach
clear and definite conclusions. Superficial agreements are quite

likely and will be numerous. When ideals are abandoned in one diocese after the other, the project will be back at the low road. One thing, however we will not get back is the present form of priesthood. It will be gone forever.

Some silence follows because all are touched by so much realism. Then there is an attempt at a reply:

I wish to thank my friend for this realistic observation. Yes, this is how life is. This danger does exist. The question is whether it should deter us from attempting this road at all or whether it should make us more careful. Should one remain on the low road because many have gradually slid down from trying the high road? The same could be said about all ideals. It could also be said to each one who attempts to become a celibate priest: "Don't you know that many have set out on the high road and gradually slid down? Remain where you are."

I think the danger exists but we can take steps to minimize it. The danger – in all the frightening details you told us – must be discussed openly during the dialog stage. But discussing it is not enough. To ensure that the dialog stage is taken seriously, a commission should be established at the bishops conference level, to send a delegation to each diocese. It will take part in those meetings of the dioceses and will eventually have to verify that the ideal of self-ministering communities is embraced genuinely and that it is safe for the diocese to move ahead. Each diocese must apply to Rome via the bishops conference for permission to move ahead, and for that permission, the statement of the delegation will be decisive.

Another NOW adherent adds:

Vague ideals are dangerous, but genuine, realistic ideals must be pursued, with all due safeguards. Our proposal is based on the realistic ideal of increased participation. When we enumerated the motives for the proposal we purposely put the shortage of priests as the last one, although in sequence of time it was the beginning of the search for a more appropriate ministry struc-

ture. Even if we had a sufficient number of priests we should
still listen to the even more urgent call for ways of becoming a
Community Church where local leaders can assume full responsibility for the gospel. This new vision of being the Church is not
yet alive everywhere, but we appeal to those areas where it is
still about to be born not to hinder others where it is already a
living reality, just as we are asking those who wish to introduce
the ordination of community leaders to do it in a way that does
not interfere with others. We must respect and help one another.
It is in this spirit that we ask for the acceptance of our proposal.

A NEVER takes up the point made:

> This is exactly why some of us ask you to withdraw your
> request. We ask you to have understanding for the situation of
> our dioceses. Our dioceses are different from yours. In our dio-
> ceses we are able to find candidates for the present type of priest-
> hood, we are able to build up a truly local Church from local
> priests. These efforts to form and encourage them will become
> very difficult or even impossible if you press ahead with your
> proposal. Out of consideration for those dioceses, please with-
> draw your request.

This plea is seen in a different way by one of those who made the
original proposal:

> The way we have formulated our proposal will allow your
> diocese to continue as in the past, while other dioceses introduce
> the two new kinds of priest. The key issue is the introduction of
> two new kinds of priest, teams of animator priests and teams of
> ordained community leaders. In this way, and only in this way, is
> the idealism of the present priests safeguarded. It is safeguarded
> both in those dioceses which go ahead in the new way and in the
> other dioceses which continue in the present way. This is why
> we have warned so strongly against introducing viri probati priests
> by way of filling gaps, because in that way you place married
> priests alongside celibate ones wherever a gap appears. The one
> is married, the other not, and that will appear as the only differ-
> ence. This is bound to cause confusion. It will also cause defec-

tions, and that will cause the uncontrollable escalation which is rightly feared by many. This disintegration would be the result of the wrong way of introducing *viri probati* priests.

The right way on the other hand is a well-planned process. It should not just escalate in an unplanned manner, nor just spill over into other dioceses. It should be introduced by communal decision where it appears feasible, and refused by communal decision where it is not yet advisable, as in the cases which were mentioned by the previous speaker. There is no need to halt the process universally because it does not suit some local situations.

Somebody resumes the NOW argument:

Mutual consideration is a duty. We have modified our proposal so as to cause the least interference in other dioceses which are at a different stage. We have to make efforts on all sides to allow dioceses to do what is best in their particular circumstances. On the one side are the dioceses which are resolved that they will not introduce ordained community leaders, or at least not at this stage. They should not be disturbed. On the other side are those who can demonstrate to us why they cannot wait any longer. They should not be hindered. There is a way of giving consideration to both. In this mutually considerate way the proposal was drawn up and we ask for its acceptance in this spirit.

The debate continues. How do you think it will end? What will your participation be in this important process?

Conclusion

The ordination of teams of community leaders gradually emerged in these pages as a possible great enrichment for the Church. Not all see it this way at present. Many have the feeling that this step would mean a deplorable, harmful development. They assume it would mean an end to the idealism with which thousands of priests are sacrificing their lives for others. They feel it would lead young people away from the spirit of self-giving which Jesus showed us. They foresee it would tempt many to choose the wide and easy road instead of the steep and narrow one to which Jesus invited us. They feel it would even mean a degree of disintegration for the Church. They feel all this would happen although they have not reflected deeper on this process.

In contrast with this, a positive and inviting picture has emerged in the pages of this book. The ordination of teams of proven Christians will mean an immense increase in the degree to which communities and their leaders can participate in the most central tasks of the Church. It will at the same time mean a deeper and more meaningful invitation for full-time priests to live the evangelical counsels in order to serve and promote this increased participation. It will mean not less spirituality but more. There will be problems but not only can they be solved but their solution will mean an enrichment of the Church.

We began this study with the observation that many urge the introduction of *viri probati* priests without seeing any problems, while others oppose it by speaking of problems which they have not reflected on. The deeper study of the question of viri probati has made us aware of several new aspects which we had not noted before. It helped us to overcome certain unreal fears which we had about this question, and also helped us to see several processes which can be helpful in introducing this new kind of priest.

Among the new aspects of which the study made us aware is the fact that there is not just one type of *viri probati* but several, and that it could be a serious mistake to choose the wrong type. We grouped the possible types into three options and saw that it is vital to choose only one of these options, the ordination of teams of community leaders and not the ordination of individuals. The first two options mean nothing more than creating substitutes for the missing full-time priests. Only the third option leads to a new way of being Church. The first two options act as a pain-killer which alleviates the symptoms of the moment but has negative side effects and does not heal. The crucial importance of choosing the third option kept re-appearing again and again: when we spoke of the vision of Church which is a stake, when we spoke about the continued commitment of the existing priests, when we considered the question of women in team ministry, and even when we spoke about the financial implications. The solution of many problems depends on making the right choice between these different types of *viri probati*.

Many will have found it surprising that an over-emphasis on the short-age of priests can have negative effects. It can mislead us to choose an approach which is narrowly interested in finding additional providers, and in this way may preserve the image of a providing ministry. The shortage should be seen and used as the trigger, not as the decisive motive.

The terminology by which we call the new kind of priest has also assumed more importance. We need a term which leads us away from the narrow focus on finding more providers. We need a term which indicates the enrichment which such a step could bring. The term "ordained commu-nity leaders" is one of the first attempts in this direction. It may not be the final choice but it indicates the direction in which we should continue searching.

Another new aspect for many of us may be that the responsibility for moving ahead is more on us than on Rome. Many are saying today that all we can do is to pray for a different top leadership of the Church. The reflections point in a different direction. We should begin by working toward a different parish wherever we are. The top leadership of the Church will change soon, but will the thousands of parishes and dioceses change soon unless we make efforts in this direction? Without substantial changes many parishes should not be allowed to have some proven leaders ordained even if it became legally possible. The task of becoming active communities is first, and it is ours.

Among the common fears with regard to the ordination of community leaders is the fear that this will lead to a loss of idealism in the Church. If these ordinations are introduced in the way proposed in this study, as the ordination of teams of local leaders, then the change will be based on more idealism, not on less. The change requires idealism on the part of the communities, on the part of those to be ordained, and very much so on the part of the animator priests. This is why we said that we need not only one new kind of priests but two, the first being the ordained community leaders and the second being the animator priests.

One of the most common fears has always been that these ordinations would lead to two classes of priests. We came to the conclusion that this would be true only for the first two options, not for the third one. Having two kinds of priest, in the form of teams of ordained community leaders and their animators, is not a problem but is part of the solution. The two kinds of priest should not be as similar as possible but actually need to be different in order to complement each other. They can only exist in mutuality.

The fear that ordinations of this kind could cause disunity in the Church is a real one. This must be feared if the process is not done correctly. What has emerged is that there are ways in which this danger can be avoided. Several helpful processes have become clearer to us, processes which reduce the shock of change, processes which avoid imposing change on others, and processes which avoid a situation where some feel that the only response possible is breaking away.

Among the helpful processes which are proposed in this study is the use of dialogue sessions in the parishes, among the priests and in the seminaries. Shock will also be reduced if parishes begin at an early stage to introduce group-conducted liturgies which prepare people for the idea of teams. A process which will also prove helpful is the publication and discussion of a "list of preconditions" to which dioceses and parishes commit themselves. It will instill the confidence that change will proceed in an orderly way and by mutual agreement, not in disarray.

The main question in the minds of bishops, priests and people is of course whether the introduction of the ordination of community leaders is feasible. The conclusion reached is a positive one. It will mean a bigger change than many thought, but it will mean an important enrichment for the Church.

What makes the change feasible is the interaction between the ordained community leaders and their animator priests. Only on this condition is it feasible. The fact that the existing priests are invited to assume the new role of animators of the teams of ordained community leaders is the key factor. This makes it possible to avoid the disintegration which the bishops feared in 1971 when they voted by a narrow margin against introducing viri probati. To introduce two new kinds of priest, not only one, is decisive. This makes it possible for one country to introduce the ordination of community leaders while the neighbouring one does not.

Only a World Synod of Bishops or a Council can undertake the task of weighing the arguments for and against, and of deciding whether or not to introduce these two new kinds of priest. Until then it is the task of dialogue and studies such as the present one to try to offer some clarifications and suggestions.

Further research is required to know the answers to questions such as: How many countries and dioceses are likely to ask for the introduction of viri probati teams? How many dioceses are likely to be ready for the processes required for introducing the ordination of community leaders? How can this be verified? How many countries are likely to retain the present ministry structure for the foreseeable future?

The recommendations outlined in this publication are open to further study and suggestions. The methodology of this kind of futuristic study necessarily involves careful reading of existing trends and calculation of how these will most probably continue to develop. Additional studies are therefore needed in order to clarify the various aspects.